P9-CCC-557

Understanding
Older Chicanas

SAGE SERIES ON
RACE AND ETHNIC RELATIONS

Series Editor:
JOHN H. STANFIELD II
University of California at Davis

This series is designed for scholars working in creative theoretical areas related to race and ethnic relations. The series will publish books and collections of original articles that critically assess and expand upon race and ethnic relations issues from American and comparative points of view.

SERIES EDITORIAL BOARD

Robert Blauner	Ruth S. Hamilton	Rebecca Morales
Jomills H. Braddock II	Dell Hymes	Chester Pierce
Scott Cummings	James Jackson	Vicki L. Ruiz
Rutledge Dennis	Roy Bryce Laporte	Gary D. Sandefur
Leonard Dinnerstein	Paul Gordon Lauren	Diana Slaughter
Reynolds Farley	William Liu	C. Matthew Snipp
Joe Feagin	Stanford M. Lyman	John Stone
Barry Glassner	Gary Marx	Bruce Williams
Steven J. Gold	Robert Miles	Melvin D. Williams

Understanding Older Chicanas

Elisa Facio

**Sage Series on Race
and Ethnic Relations**

v o l u m e   14

SAGE Publications
International Educational and Professional Publisher
Thousand Oaks   London   New Delhi

Copyright © 1996 by Sage Publications, Inc.

All rights reserved. No part of this book may be reproduced or utilized in any form or by any means, electronic or mechanical, including photocopying, recording, or by any information storage and retrieval system, without permission in writing from the publisher.

For information address:

SAGE Publications, Inc.
2455 Teller Road
Thousand Oaks, California 91320
E-mail: order@sagepub.com

SAGE Publications Ltd.
6 Bonhill Street
London EC2A 4PU
United Kingdom

SAGE Publications India Pvt. Ltd.
M-32 Market
Greater Kailash I
New Delhi 110 048 India

Printed in the United States of America

Library of Congress Cataloging-in-Publication Data

Facio, Elisa.
    Understanding older Chicanas: Sociological and policy
perspectives / Elisa Facio.
        p.   cm. — (Sage series on race and ethnic relations; v. 14)
    Includes bibliographical references (p.   ) and index.
    ISBN 0-8039-4580-9 (Cloth : alk. paper). — ISBN 0-8039-4581-7
(pbk.: alk. paper)
    1. Mexican American aged women.   2. Mexican American aged
women—California, Northern—Case studies.   I. Title.   II. Series.
E184.M5F33   1995
305.26'089'687273—dc20   95-9291

This book is printed on acid-free paper.

96 97 98 99 00 10 9 8 7 6 5 4 3 2 1

Sage Typesetter: Christina M. Hill

CONTENTS

Series Editor's Introduction

This is a fascinating qualitative study of Chicana elderly. In excellent form, Elisa Facio uses participant-observation and oral history techniques to reconstruct the addends, gender roles, and lives of Chicanas in a home for the elderly. She also offers valuable insights about the problems and paradoxes in doing insider qualitative research. In that sense, her reflective sociologocal style is just as important as the superb substantive points she draws from her data.

JOHN H. STANFIELD II

1

Introduction

The aged drew serious attention from policymakers as well as from scholars during the 1930s (Markides & Mindel, 1987). At that time, increased life expectancy and declining fertility had led to increasing numbers of older people. The hardships of the Great Depression also made the aged more visible (Markides & Mindel, 1987, p. 10). The introduction of social security in 1935 and institutionalized retirement at age 65 helped make the aged an "emerging social problem," a perception that began in the early 1900s (Fischer, 1978, p. 68).

Coupled with this increased visibility of the aged as a social problem has been the growth of social gerontological research since the 1930s, at an accelerating pace. The number and proportion of older people, as well as number of people who have retired, usually at the age of 65, continue to increase. Although much of this retirement has been voluntary, many older people have been forced from their jobs by mandatory retirement provisions (Markides & Mindel, 1987, p. 10).

Changes in the family also helped make the aged more visible as a social problem. With industrialization, urbanization, and widespread geographic mobility of the population, the elderly in the second half of the 20th century could no longer expect to live with their children or to be supported by them if they needed help. Most elderly, of course, would not want such arrangements; they would rather be independent, despite their limited resources.

Consistent with a social problems orientation, social gerontological research places major focus on adaptation and adjustment to old age (Maddox & Riley, 1976). For example, research has focused on life satisfaction, morale, psychological well-being, adjustment, and adaptation or "successful" aging. There is, of course, increased interest in other

1

aspects of the aging process, such as retirement and widowhood. But much of this interest involves how these aspects affect the process of adjustment to old age.

Social gerontology explicitly or implicitly made a value judgment, a value judgment that has been consistent with the growth of the welfare state since the 1930s: "Older people, more than other people, have been seen by scholars and policymakers as requiring adjustment to their stage in the life cycle" (Markides & Mindel, 1987, p. 10). Much of the research has also suggested that older people needed help to do this, with much of the help coming from the state. Basically, research has focused on the aged from a social service or needs assessment approach. The bulk of social gerontology research emphasizes the lack of social services such as medical care, Medicaid, and welfare.

Torres-Gil (1992) has described the 60 years between 1930 and 1990 as the Modern Aging Period.[1] According to Torres-Gil, during this time, new forms of government intervention and provision for the aged were established. Age became a determining factor in policy making and in the distribution of services, as well as contributing to the emergence of "senior-citizen interest groups and an 'aging enterprise' comprised of providers and professionals to serve a growing elderly population" (p. 1).

CHICANO AGING RESEARCH
AND THE MODERN AGING PERIOD

The growth of the aging enterprise took place with limited attention to ethnicity and minority-group status. It was not until the 1960s that notable studies of older African Americans appeared (Markides & Mindel, 1987). Attention to Latinos came even later, during the 1970s. Most of this attention was given to Chicanos, who constitute the largest proportion of Latinos. In one of the few major publications on older Chicanos, Gebler, Moore, and Guzman (1970) noted that "Mexican Americans in this country have so many serious problems that the difficulties of the aged have attracted little attention" (p. 32). Although Chicanos have been the subject of research investigations for some time, interest in older Chicanos is only recent. Publications focusing exclusively on the older segment of the Chicano population are few, a fact that may indeed confirm that Chicanos as a group have too many problems for the aged to receive much attention, as Gebler et al. asserted. However, Markides,

Martin, & Gomez (1983) stated, "those familiar with older Chicanos, will testify that their problems are far more pronounced than those of the general Chicano population" (p. 1).

Social scientists gave little attention to older Chicanos in part because of misconceptions and stereotypes about their place in society and the family, misperceptions that continue today. Much of the social science literature has painted a rather romanticized picture of the extended Chicano family, which has been thought to support and protect the aged from a "hostile" world. As a result, the problems of elderly Chicanos, unlike their counterparts in some other racial/ethnic groups, were thought to be minimized by the "supportive qualities" of the Chicano family. Recently, this position has attracted critical attention.[2]

The lack of research attention to older Chicanos may also reflect their limited political power (Markides et al., 1983, p. 1). Many of them are not U.S. citizens, even though they have lived in this country for many years. Many have little or no education and face economic, cultural, and linguistic barriers that limit their political participation. Also, they form a smaller minority of the total Chicano population than the elderly in other groups. As a whole, "Chicanos along with other Latino groups (Puerto Ricans, Cubans, etc.) historically have been ignored or considered as insignificant by social scientists and policy makers" (Maldonado, 1979, p. 176).

Changing Expectations of Chicano Old Age

During the Modern Aging Period, research on aging among Chicanos overwhelmingly focused on changing expectations and adaptation to relocation. Much of the aged population grew up in conditions and family contexts very different from the present. For this generation, the word *familia* meant an extended, multigenerational group of people, among whom specific social roles were ascribed. Mutual support, sustenance, and interaction among family members during both work and leisure hours dominated the lives of these traditional Chicano families.

Elderly members of traditional, extended families were presumably spared many of the hazards to physical and psychological well-being usually associated with disengagement from active working roles. Adult children provided economic support and assistance with housekeeping for men and women too old to continue working. At the same time, because grandparents were given specific social roles to perform, older persons continued to be valued family members. Their expertise and importance as role models gave them status and authority; they were highly respected by younger family members and played key roles in the upkeep of the house and providing of child care (Maldonado, 1975). There is evidence today that Chicanos, more than other ethnic groups, continue to have an extended-family orientation (Baca Zinn, 1991; Keefe, Padilla, & Carlos, 1979). Analyses of data on elderly residents of Los Angeles show that African Americans and Anglos generally conform to dominant Anglo family patterns (i.e., the nuclear family), whereas Chicano elderly both live differently and have different expectations and opinions about familism (i.e., stronger commitment to extended family relationships; Bengston & Burton, 1980).

Although some findings confirmed the idea that the extended Chicano family, supportive of its elderly, continued to operate in the United States, a second group of investigations provided contradictory evidence. For example, both Maldonado (1975) and Nunez (1975) concluded that rapid social change was breaking down the traditional extended family and that as a consequence, older Chicanos (as well as Anglos) were experiencing isolation and alienation. Maldonado (1975) argued that as younger generations of Chicanos rose in social status, they became more mobile, increasing the physical distance between themselves and their kin, which also decreased familial interdependence. Urbanization, modernization, and increased acculturation among young Chicanos also tended to strengthen nuclear ties and weaken links to extended family members. Hence, "Latino elders may increasingly find themselves alone in an alien culture without the type of support they value and expect" (Becerra, 1983, p. 110).

The available facts support neither those who contend that traditional familial living patterns are a thing of the past nor those who claim that extended, supportive family structures still exist for a majority of U.S. Latinos. According to Becerra (1983),

> For, on the one hand, while urbanization is making the traditional paradigm untenable for many older Chicanos today, the evidence suggests that rather than disappearing completely, the extended family structure is being modified to fit changing economic, social, and cultural conditions. (p. 115)

Moreover, the extremes of the very traditional and the very modern continue to exist alongside changing familial patterns. It is unclear how many older Chicanos are faced with these transitions; however, a proportion of this aged cohort probably faces change, with all its implications for their old age.

Furthermore, Becerra (1983) argued the great majority of Chicano elders were, and continue to be, less acculturated than their children and grandchildren. They still maintain role expectations that more closely resemble traditional cultural roles. Thus, the interaction of modern and traditional values can present a very stressful and conflictual situation for the aged. The elderly are unique in the sense that they have experienced immigration from Mexico and a transition from rural to urban settings.

Adaptation to Relocation

Most older Chicanos have had to adapt to two major relocations: the move from Mexico to the United States and the shift from a rural to urban setting (Becerra, 1983, p. 108). Historically, several factors encouraged movement across the border to the United States:

1. The dissolution of the peonage system in Mexico as a result of the success of the 1910 Revolution enabled farm laborers to leave to seek work on farms in the American Southwest.
2. The completion of railroad connections to the Mexican interior provided a means of transportation to the U.S. border for workers from densely populated, impoverished areas in central Mexico.
3. The introduction of capital and labor-intensive irrigation farming to the Southwest created a demand for seasonal wage labor (Becerra, 1983, p. 108).

The movement from rural Mexico to the rural Southwest represented only a modest cultural shock for Mexican emigrants, because they tended to work and live in ethnically homogeneous settings. These communities were minimally influenced by Anglo culture and provided support for traditional Mexican familial structures, which emphasized the elderly male's role as an authority in agricultural skills and the elderly female's importance in child rearing (Sanchez-Ayendez, 1984). This rural heritage shared by most of today's Latino elderly came to an end, however, with the increasing mechanization of agriculture, the Bracero Program of seasonal labor, and the movement of rural populations to urban areas.

Today, 85% to 90% of all Chicanos, including almost all elderly Chicanos, reside in urban areas. Some Latino gerontologists see the urbanization of Mexican Americans as the more disruptive relocation for the Chicano elderly. Thus, the focus of much research has been on those areas of Chicano life that some scholars suggest are undergoing change as a result of urbanization and hence may present problems for the older Chicano (Becerra, 1983, p. 109).

Despite much speculation, understanding of the factors that shape their aged lives is limited. The focus of Chicano aging research has reflected social gerontology in general: how social change affected *adjustment.* But what is old age like for the Chicano? Because of many changes, older Chicanos may find themselves defining new roles for themselves, roles that add to or replace traditional roles. Generally, such questions remain inadequately addressed.

Approaches used in Chicano family literature are rooted in modernization theory or governed by traditional paradigms. Chicano aging studies have illustrated more concern with evolutionary changes in family structure, which are assumed to occur with acculturation, and their impact on the aged. It must be noted, however, that a major contribution of Chicano aging studies is their discussion of culture. Nonetheless, there are problems with the treatment of the concept; for example, gender differences in the aging process are explained solely by culture. Now that society is moving into the "New Aging" Period, research agendas concerned with questions of structural changes and the subsequent responses of the aged population, and society as a whole, lead to new directions in gerontological research.

OLDER CHICANOS AND
THE "NEW AGING PERIOD"

Torres-Gil (1992) argued that the Modern Aging Period has ended and that the 1990s marked the onset of the New Aging Period. Changes in the social, economic, and political fabric of American society demand altered views of the aged population and the manner in which government and society will provide for them. According to Torres-Gil,

> At present, the United States is at a crossroads similar to that faced in the 1920s. In comparison to other nations, the U.S. appears to be succeeding economically and politically, although severe social dislocation exists as evidenced by homelessness, crime, drugs, inner-city turmoil, and a health and educational system in crisis. (p. 6)

Aging and the increasing number of older people will bring these problems to the surface, forcing society to take on the question of responsibility for those less fortunate: the elderly poor, older women, ethnic minorities, those who live in rural areas, and frail older people. Torres-Gil (1992) described the New Aging Period as a time

> that will witness change in the image of the elderly due, in large part, to generational claims, diversity, and longevity. This new image will directly affect both the political and policy decisions in financing benefits to the elderly and our preparedness for their future cohorts. (p. 9)

This study does not address how these three distinct forces shape the lives of older Chicanos, in particular older Chicanas. Rather, it serves as a case in point that lends support to turning our focus to a diversifying elderly population. Also, this study examines how older Chicanas view and define their old age as society moves into the New Aging Period. Thus, this research provides important information about a small but significant subgroup of society's diverse elderly population, which, in turn, may broaden our knowledge of older ethnic women as we approach the 21st century.

Today racial/ethnic minorities make up 14% of the population over age 65. Minorities include a smaller proportion of elderly and a larger proportion of younger adults than the Anglo population. In 1990, 13% of Anglos, 8% of African Americans, and 6% of Latinos were age 65 and older (Tauber, 1993). The difference results primarily from higher rates of fertility and higher mortality rates among the non-white population under age 65 than among the white population under 65. However, beginning in the early part of the 21st century, the proportion of older people is expected to increase at a higher rate for the non-white population than for the white population, partly because of the large proportion of children in these groups who, unlike their parents and especially their grandparents, are expected to reach old age. By 2020, 22% of the older population is projected to be non-white; by 2050, 32% will be non-white (U.S. Bureau of the Census, 1989). The number of minority elderly is growing more rapidly than the number of European American elderly, with the most rapid growth occurring within Chicano/Latino and Asian populations (Stanford & Yee, 1991). These population shifts will be even more dramatic in places such as California, where 40% of the older population will be ethnic minorities by 2020 (Torres-Gil & Hyde, 1990).

Following African Americans, Latinos are the largest U.S. racial/ ethnic minority population, with over 85% concentrated in metropolitan areas. They are also the fastest-growing population in the United States (Torres-Gil, 1986). Between 1970 and 1980, the number of older Latinos in the United States increased by 74%, compared to a 25% increase in the population of all elderly. Latinos include many groups, each with its own distinct national/cultural heritage: Mexicans, Puerto Ricans, Cubans, Central and South Americans, and U.S.-born Mexican Americans, or Chicanos, whose history in the United States predates settlement by English-speaking groups. Although bonded by a common language, these groups differ substantially in terms of geographic concentration, income, and education. Chicanos are the largest but poorest group, constituting 64% of the Latino population and concentrated in five primarily rural southwestern states.[3]

Compared to Anglos and to other ethnic minorities, the Spanish-speaking population is a youthful group, with a median age of 23.2 years, 7 years younger than the norm in the United States (Lacayo, 1982). Only 3.5% of this population is 65 years of age and over, a figure that has been stable over the past decade (U.S. Bureau of the Census, 1991). A number of factors underlie the relative youthfulness of the Latino population. One variable is its lower average life expectancy. The most important contributing factor, however, is the generally high fertility rate. The number of children born and the average family size exceed the national average. Immigration and repatriation patterns are secondary factors, with the youngest, and often poorest, people most likely to move to a new country, and some middle-aged and older Mexicans moving back to Mexico (Markides et al., 1983; Torres-Gil, 1986).

Despite its relative youthfulness, the Latino population experienced the greatest increase in median age of all racial/ethnic groups between 1960 and 1990. This suggests that the percentage of older Latinos may rise steeply in the future, as younger cohorts reach old age. Nevertheless, given the higher fertility rate, the proportion of elderly among Latinos will remain well below that of the total U.S. population.

Gender distinctions among Latinos are similar to those of other groups of elderly. Women live longer and outnumber men, more often remaining widowed and living alone than men do. Older Latino men marry or remarry more often than men in other racial/ethnic minority groups; 83% of older Latino men are married, but only 33% of older Latinas live with a spouse (Lacayo, 1982).

A major reason for gerontological research and practice to take account of older women's needs is that they form the fastest-growing segment of the population. The aging society is primarily a female one. Women represent 56% of the population age 65 to 74 and 72% of those over age 85.[4] Older women are more likely than older men to be poor; to have inadequate retirement income; to be widowed, divorced, and alone; and to be caregivers to other relatives. Despite greater social problems, many older women display resilience and innovativeness in the face of adversity.

WHO ARE THE CHICANO ELDERLY?

We're old, but we're very proud of who we are, we have a beautiful culture, we're Mexicans, not Americans. . . . We were raised here in both cultures, but we're still Mexicans.

—Gloria Rios, 76

Aged Chicanos would probably refrain from using the term *Chicano* as a means of self-identity. Rather, they seem to prefer *Mexicano* or *Mexican*. Other acceptable terms are Mexican American or Spanish-speaking (Maldonado, 1979, p. 175). By preferring these identity terms, the elderly do not mean to disassociate themselves from those who call themselves Chicanos. Rather, the preference reflects the Mexican nationality of most elderly, their strong identity with Mexican culture, and the relative newness of Chicano as a general term of identification. For purposes of this study, the terms *Chicano elder(s)* and *older Chicanos* will be used interchangeably.

Older Chicanos are people of Mexican origin, including those who were born in Mexico and immigrated to the United States, about 58% of the present older Chicano population (Maldonado, 1979, p. 177). Many of these older people immigrated as children or youths between 1910 and 1930 as a result of the Mexican revolution and the need for labor in the United States.

These immigrants compose an important element of today's older Chicanos. The fact that they arrived in the United States as youngsters and were nurtured by adults who were products of Mexican society has certain cultural consequences for these Chicano elders. That they were reared by poor undocumented workers has had tremendous socioeconomic consequences, as well (Maldonado, 1979, p. 177).

A second subgroup of Mexican-born Chicano elders includes those who immigrated as adults. Undocumented immigration has been difficult to measure. However, legal immigration statistics indicate a significant increase of Mexican immigration beginning in 1953. Because most Mexican immigration is labor-oriented, it can be assumed (although data are extremely limited) that adults constitute a very important proportion of this immigrant population. Just what their proportion is among the Chicano elder Mexican-born population is unknown, but it is not expected to be near that of young arrivals. Nevertheless, this subpopulation would tend to be culturally quite different from those who arrived decades earlier. These elders have had less time to prepare for their old age in this society, including less time for socialization and building economic and cognitive bases.

The third subgroup of older Chicanos includes those who were born and reared in this country and are thus natives. They represent about 42% of today's Chicano elder population (Maldonado, 1979, p. 177). Many of these older Chicanos constitute a third generation and trace their roots to the original settlers. This is especially true in New Mexico, Arizona, and Colorado.

OLDER CHICANAS

Ironically, Chicano aging has been viewed as a uniform process. Minority and Chicano aging research has failed to critically address the lives of older Chicanas. In minority aging, women's issues have been addressed using a needs-assessment approach. In Chicano aging research, the plight of older women has been masked with notions of familism. *Familism,* as defined in Chicano aging literature, embraces cultural values of family unity and expected mutual aid, respect for the aged, and a positive gender hierarchy considered specific to Chicano families.[5] The concept of familism has been used to explain the status of the elderly, how they cope with aging, and how gender dynamics among the elderly are constructed.

Over the last two decades, studies guided by the concept of familism have described characteristics of strength and vitality among older Chicanas, who nonetheless defer to their husbands and male relatives (Boone, 1980; Coles, 1989; Sanchez-Ayendez, 1986; Sotomayor, 1973). Generally, older Chicanas have been viewed from a traditional perspective where gender differences are neither challenged nor questioned

(Alvirez, Bean, & William, 1981; Mirande & Enriquez, 1979). Within this perspective, the older Chicana has been described as the expressive individual in the family. More specifically, the role of the Chicana grandmother has been portrayed as the nurturing elder, child care provider, and facilitator of religious and cultural values (Boswell & Curtis, 1984; Fitzpatrick, 1971; Perez, 1986).

Older Chicanas have been overwhelmingly portrayed as focal individuals in the extended family. Households have formed largely around women, mainly because of their role in child care. Alignments between women, both within the family and outside of it, often constitute the core of family networks. Scholars claim that older women perform a variety of tasks for their families (Markides, Boldt, & Ray, 1986; Schmidt & Padilla, 1983).

The Chicano family has been portrayed as a strong, resourceful unit with the Chicana as its center. For example, according to Zepeda (1979), "The role of 'la abuela' (grandmother) in the family is something most Mexicanos/Chicanos treasure" (p. 5). Notably, Chicana grandmothers have been considered "the backbone of family endurance and the symbol of cultural survival" (Zepeda, p. 12). The stories of two women embody these values:

> Louisa . . . is the matriarch of her family. A woman with strong ideas and a wealth of practical knowledge, she is regarded as the family advice giver and chief storyteller.

> At 56, Esperanza Salcido has always planned her life around her family. Her children are grown now, but her work of caring for others has changed very little. Today she looks after her young grandchildren. "Recently my dad got sick," she said, "so I'm taking care of him, too. . . . Yes, it's hard sometimes, but that's what families are all about." (Elsasser, MacKenzie, & Tixier y Vigil, 1980, pp. 18, 62)

Social scientists have interpreted the role of older Chicanas as active and dominant. Chicanas appear to play an increasingly dominant role in the extended family as they grow older. Some scholars note that this contradicts the myth that the Chicano family is a patriarchal structure. This paradox has been explained by Maldonado (1975) as the consequence of high early death rates among Chicanos. Others attempt to explain it by simply noting that women weather the transition into old age better than men do. Male roles are seen as more tenuous and less well-defined, providing fewer opportunities for older men to make themselves useful in their families in nontraditional, noneconomic ways (Cuellar, 1978; Velez, 1978).

This perspective implies that the older Chicana's subordinate status is vital for the physical and cultural survival of the family. Hence, for advocates of this approach, the cultural continuity of the Chicano family appears to be embedded in the Chicana's domestic and caregiving role. The continuity of the life course for older Chicanas is interpreted as remaining family-centered. Whether familism is conceptualized as a structural, cultural, or a combined phenomenon, studies consistently project the family as the most, and many times the only, important force in the lives of older Chicanas.

Rather than considering familism largely as an empirical or structural phenomenon, this concept must also be conceptualized as an ideological force. Casting familism as an ideology would help redefine the study of older Chicanas in broader sociological terms. In other words, it is important to look to ideology to understand where familism is rooted with respect to class, race/ethnicity, gender, and culture. To do this, we must identify the ideological components associated with familism and older Chicanas.

My findings refute the empirical evidence in Chicano aging literature. First, let us refer to the notion of the multigenerational household or extended family. In the lives of my respondents, familism as an empirical phenomenon—manifestations of expected mutual aid and support—appears to have changed, although certain elements of familism, namely family unity, have remained.

In other words, the multigenerational household and extended family do not operate as the literature would lead us to believe. My findings suggest that older Chicanas have established modified networks with other older Chicanas and not necessarily with their own family. They still value family unity, but this unity may stem not from familism or culture but from gender and age dynamics. Thus, the data call for broadening our conceptualization of social networks among older Chicanas according to age and gender.

Second, the application of familism in explaining the gender hierarchy associated with the aged is the most ambiguous and limiting discussion in Chicano aging literature. In order to get a clearer sense of this hierarchy, we need to explore those aspects of familism that are rooted in gender. Studies by Pesquera (1985) and Segura (1986) have illustrated that motherhood and male authority are considered ideological components of familism, along with family unity. Male authority or patriarchy bonds women to motherhood and family caregiving roles (Segura, 1986, p. 199). The ideology of familism values these roles as beneficial to the maintenance of the family. The value placed on motherhood continues with the transition to grandmotherhood. In other words, the values associated with motherhood legitimate the status of grandmotherhood. What we then have is the continued reproduction of gender. How older Chicanas respond to grandmotherhood is interesting. My findings suggest that older Chicanas found grandmotherhood "confining" and limiting" and that they sought ways to avoid meeting the expectations associated with grandmotherhood. Many of the women interviewed expressed joy and pride in being grandmothers, but they were not willing to take on the expectations associated with grandmotherhood, namely, child care. Thus, a clearer identification of the values and expectations associated with the ideological component of familism and older Chicana lives is in order.

Male authority becomes a complex issue as many of these women are widows and no longer have to deal with male authority at home as they did earlier. Undoubtedly, however, interactions with male relatives and male individuals in various settings take on a particular character shaped by patriarchy. In addition, the value that patriarchy places on motherhood and grandmotherhood appears to manifest itself during the Chicana's later years.

This discussion leads me to look further at gender. Such an analysis, no doubt, will illuminate the ideological premises and underlying implications of familism, namely, the value of male authority over females. However, this is not specific to Chicano families. Nonetheless, gender is a major component or dynamic of Chicano familism that continues to manifest itself throughout the Chicana's life course. Familism as proposed in Chicano aging literature has only served to explain and understand women as wives, mothers, and grandmothers.

This work is concerned with a group of women whose lives are no longer solely centered in the family. It focuses on older Chicanas who are no longer married, who no longer mother in their family of procreation, or who are not involved in traditional family networks. Theoretically, it is important to stop "lumping" married and unmarried women together as if all women were alike. This analytical separation allows for a better understanding of older Chicana lives, as many no longer directly identify themselves in relationship to a traditional family structure. In other words, the lives of older Chicanas encompass much more than simply family relationships.

As a means of *transcending* the limited focus of familism, rather than rejecting the concept completely, sociological approaches such as political economy and feminist theory are considered. The political economy approach generally takes the structural forces of social organization as its level of analysis. Rather than looking to individuals or technology as primary causal forces in society, political economy is ultimately concerned with the social relations of production (Alford & Friedland, 1985). The aged, in a political economy analysis, are a group of people who are used in helping to stabilize the capitalist mode of production by regulating the workforce and maximizing productivity (Minkler & Estes, 1991).

Chicanos have also been analyzed as fulfilling the needs of capitalism by occupying low-wage jobs in a segmented labor force (Almaguer, 1975; Barrera, 1979). The political economy approach helps to illustrate how older Chicanos are influenced by the political and economic position that Chicanos have historically held in the production process. Also, political economy analysis focuses on social power and inequality. This changes the focus of study from how individuals can adapt to aging to what political and economic changes can optimize the aging process.

Furthermore, a political economy analysis of older Chicanos provides an understanding of how the Chicano family is shaped by its position in the system of production. This perspective highlights how the role of the elder in the family results from the economic exploitation of Chicanos, showing how the family mediates capitalism and aging.

Feminist theories vary as to whether the central social force that creates social differentiation based on gender is patriarchy, capitalism, or both. Theorists who use an analysis of patriarchy describe and explain how male dominance has been practiced historically under different social and economic systems. Early Marxist feminism describes how women as a group had a definite relationship to the means of production and how their place in the home was economically necessary for the operation of a capitalist system. Later Marxist feminism has brought the consideration of patriarchy back into the analysis, looking at the dynamic relation between women's work in the home and productive forces outside of the home. Both capitalists as a class and men as a class are seen to benefit from the social relations of patriarchy and capitalism.

Feminist theory could draw studies of older Chicanos away from a concern with how the structure and functions of the family benignly benefit the elderly and toward an identification of how gender and class dominance transcends the family and continues into old age. Under feminist theory, Chicana grandmothers would be more than matriarchs; they would also take their place as players in the historical and societal process of gender oppression.

In general, the present generation of older Chicanas has been socialized to assume traditional tasks of child care and household maintenance. For many women of this generation, school was a luxury and a privilege. In this study, many women stressed how much they wanted to attend school. However, their parents, in particular their fathers, did not see the long-term benefits but only the immediate necessity of their labor. The "real" skills they were expected to need when they were no longer girls were those they learned at home.

Women's work consisted of growing and preparing food, making children's school clothes, and teaching children the hymns and prayers of the church. (The Catholic church held and continues to hold a special importance in the lives of many older Chicanas.) They learned to deliver babies and treat illnesses with herbs and patience. In almost every town, one or two women, in addition to working in their homes, served other families in the community as *curanderas* (healers) or *parteras* (midwives).

During the childhood of today's elderly Chicanas, grandparents were a vital part of the family. Many women lived with their grandparents, where they were culturally educated with respect to food, traditional customs and beliefs, and the struggles that relatives experienced during and after the Mexican Revolution. By an early age, most older Chicanas had married, going straight from their fathers' to their husbands' homes. They moved from being daughters to being wives and mothers, with little, if any, time in between. Some of these women tell of early married life where they played games (e.g., skipping rope) with their girlfriends while cooking a pot of beans.

Older Chicanas in general find themselves struggling with past traditions in the midst of contemporary realities, creating contradictions and challenges in their old age. They were socialized with certain ideas about old age: that it would bring harmony, status, respect, and solace. However, the reality of their present lives (poverty, family structural changes, differential life expectancies, longevity) calls for the aged to reassess their expectations and thus redefine their old age. Older Chicanas, in particular, must also deal with traditions that reinforce a gender hierarchy. This is one aspect of older Chicana lives that has not been critically examined.

In the preceding discussion, I have attempted to introduce readers to older Chicanas, both past and present. This brief introduction touches on their early socialization regarding old age and subsequently their particular expectations about growing old. Given the realities of their present lives and their expectations of old age, what are the challenges that confront older Chicanas in socially constructing their old age? In other words, what is their social, economic, and cultural context? This study argues that old age for Chicanas is largely determined by structural and cultural constraints. Structurally, older Chicanas are placed in poverty. Culturally, they are prescribed to remain without companionship and as caretakers. In other words, they are consigned to grandmotherhood. Older Chicanas, however, have taken measures to deal with conflicting cultural traditions and structural constraints through community organizations, such as senior citizen centers and the church, and their own families. Within these contexts, older Chicanas have actively defined or constructed varied meanings of their old age, their womanhood.

The discussion begins in Chapter 2 with a detailed description and introduction to the social world of older Chicanas. This chapter looks to the participation of Chicanas in a senior citizen center, which provides a means of confronting the contradictions and challenges of old age. For example, this discussion examines how older Chicanas have accommodated to old age by developing strategies to deal with particular concerns of self-worth, economic subsistence, and cultural concerns of *respeto*. More important, the senior center is pivotal in the older Chicana's pursuit of her old-age identity. The center represents a space that allows older Chicanas to exert a sense of control over the aging process and to protect any means of independence they have acquired.

Chapter 3 turns to the structural or economic constraints that influence the meaning of old age for Chicanas. I argue that poverty largely shapes the lives of these women. The issue of poverty or economic vulnerability is not specific to older Chicanas. Generally, for older women, poverty is largely attributed to a strict division of labor by gender in both the home and labor market. The purpose of this chapter is to understand what contributes to the older Chicana's poverty and to look at the limited options available to her in constructing her old age. This discussion is largely guided by a gender analysis, with limited attention given to class and racial/ethnic oppression.

Given their poverty and the cultural value of familism, namely respeto, older Chicanas develop a complex relationship with their children. Chapter 4 describes these relationships and how changing familial structures affect the older Chicana's perception of herself and old age. Given limited resources, physical vulnerability, and the interdependent relationship between older Chicanas and their families, the social construction of old age primarily takes place within the very institution of the family. Thus, I argue that familial relationships between older Chicanas and their children are largely shaped by economic status, or poverty, familism, and gender. This appears to be a distinguishing feature of aging for older Chicanas.

Chapter 5 focuses on the cultural expectations or constraints older Chicanas face in constructing their old age, or womanhood, within the institution of the family and the larger Chicano community. I argue that Chicano culture requires that older women, whether they are biological or surrogate grandmothers, conform to the role of caregivers. Generally, cultural norms discourage older Chicanas from seeking male companionship but steer them toward an old age spent as caregivers, more commonly known as *la abuela*. However, older Chicanas desire to be more than simply grandmothers, as currently proposed by the Chicano community. Older Chicanas also want to establish their identities as cultural teachers and older women. The cultural context of aging, primarily familism or respeto and cultural values of women as caregivers or nurturers, is analyzed. In this chapter, we clearly see how familism, ageism, and gender influence the Chicana's social definition of old age.

In sum, I aim to provide a feminist perspective of the socioeconomic conditions of older Chicana lives with an interpretation of their cultural expressions. Such an approach involves a critique of cultural, political, and economic conditions in the United States. It is influenced by the tradition of advocacy scholarship, which challenges the claims of "objectivity" and links research to community concerns and social change. The approach is driven by a passion to place the Chicana, as speaking subject, at the center of intellectual discourse (de la Torre & Pesquera, 1993). It does not ignore the fact that older Chicana "voices" are influenced by class, race, gender, and sexuality. The experiences associated with voice "must be situated within a framework that recognizes the influence of race, class, and gender on group experience" (Andersen & Collins, 1994, p. xiii). Nor does this study ignore that the inclusion of "silenced people" is crucial for comprehensive analyses of class, race, gender, and sexuality.

The traditional intellectual enterprise compels Chicana scholarship to stretch disciplinary boundaries, discover new methodologies, and formulate new directions in theory building, in order to comprehend the

Chicana's complex position in a society stratified along lines of class, race/ethnicity, gender, and sexuality. Such an approach is vital in maintaining our presence in our own disciplines, our historical roots in Chicano studies, our academic and political interest in women's studies and feminist theory, and our own "protected" space.

This work *defines* and *describes* the parameters under which older Chicanas/Mexicanas socially construct the meaning of old age. It is an attempt to understand the meaning older Chicanas attribute to their total life situations. Much of the data may seem obvious. For example, older Chicanas experience widowhood and grandmotherhood as other women and women of color do. However, this study provides an analysis of how familism and gender simultaneously structure individual and collective experiences for older Chicanas.

Furthermore, this study avoids the social problems approach characteristic of gerontological research (Andersen & Collins, 1994; Stoller & Gibson, 1994). Studies of oppressed groups, particularly people of color, usually generate thoughts of how individuals are victimized and oppressed by societal institutions or systems. Indeed many social problems are linked to class, race, gender, and sexual orientation. But the social problems approach ignores the independent views people have of themselves and the society in which they live. The following study illustrates that older Chicanas are not just victims, but also creative actors in negotiating the dialectic of aging and womanhood.

I view this work as part of a larger collective effort in illuminating the voices of Chicanas, which historically have not been chronicled and thus were rendered invisible (de la Torre & Pesquera, 1993). In spite of the academic claims of value-free inquiry, Chicanas have not been deemed worthy of study. When they have been studied, stereotypes and distortions have prevailed. Also, I view this study as challenging the Eurocentric male bias of "detached," "value-free" inquiry, an underlying premise of traditional disciplines. Thus, the goal of this book is threefold:

1. To provide an understanding of the aging process for Chicanas through older Chicana voices
2. To contribute theoretical insight regarding the simultaneity of familism and gender in older Chicana lives
3. To provide important data about older Chicanas for public policy making as society enters the New Aging Period

The remainder of this chapter discusses the fieldwork process.

FIELDWORK PROCESS

This study took place in a northern California suburban area with a population close to half a million. The city is an agricultural service sector with light industry such as food processing. The government sector has largely contributed to the city's urban growth over the last 10 years. Information for this study was collected at a senior citizen center in one of the city's Chicano neighborhoods.

Initially, I tried to generate a sample according to traditional methods and standards of the social sciences. The researcher is expected to seek out random samples. Contacting credible associations, agencies, and community organizations has been established as a way to locate legitimate resources or contacts. However, this criterion assumes equality in accessibility to populations. In other words, seeking out a sample consisting of a nontraditional group such as older Chicanas is not a straightforward task. Thus the "purposeful" character of this sample was established prior to the actual selection process and built into it.[6] In order to explore Chicana old age, I relied on my own personal judgment in selecting an appropriate sample, sometimes referred to as a purposeful sample (see Pesquera, 1985, pp. 32-33).

My foremost concern was to generate a sample of older Chicanas who were physically and mentally capable of taking part in the project. Accessibility was another issue that influenced my decision to seek potential participants from senior citizens' centers and the Catholic church. This decision eliminated much work in generating a sample from social agencies and professional associations that act only as referral and "selective" data centers. I had access to many such agencies; however, many of them were ill-informed about older Chicanos. Therefore, I sought information on services allocated to older Chicanos from agencies that dealt specifically with the Chicano community (Tobias, 1987).

After contacting the major social agency serving the Chicano community, I was informed that there were two senior citizens centers serving the Chicano aged in the county. I chose to generate a sample from the senior center that specifically met social and nutritional needs of older Chicanos. I also selected this site because it had a long-standing reputation for providing services aimed at the older Chicano population. This senior citizens center (which I will refer to simply as the Center) was primarily funded for nutritional and transportation services.

I contacted the Center director to discuss the possibility of my conducting research there. Fortunately, the Center director was an invaluable contact and resource person. She voiced her awareness and concern about the problems faced by older Chicanos and about the limited amount of research addressing these issues. After this brief meeting, she granted me permission to pursue my investigation. In order to become familiar with the Center and its members, I asked to work as a volunteer. My responsibilities included keeping daily attendance records, collecting money for noon meals, and leading exercise classes three times a week. Once a certain rapport had been established, I proceeded to select respondents for life histories.

My intention was to interview about 30 to 35 older Chicanas. Eligibility of potential respondents was determined on the basis of three criteria determined by the research design. Respondents were to be female, 60 years old or older, and of Mexican ethnic identity, born in Mexico or the United States. Marital status was not a determining factor in the selection process, given that more than 95% of the women in this age bracket were widows.

The method of selecting respondents for the study depended largely on personal rapport. It was not until I had completed 7 months of participant observation that I felt comfortable and competent to ask selected women for their participation in the recording of a life history. Again, based on personal rapport, I intentionally sought out those women I felt would agree to be interviewed. Given that I intended to collect 30 to 35 life histories, and that I sought the most accurate, free-flowing, and intimate accounts possible, I spent a tremendous amount of time and energy in trying to establish a sense of trust with as many older Chicanas as possible.

The Politics of Research

Race and gender relations had a definite impact on my research. For example, my being a Chicana affected the reception I received and the data to which I had access. Also, researchers of color who study their own communities are "outsiders" owing to the class divide. Stanfield and Dennis (1993) state, "The class gap between the researcher of color and subjects of color, who are more than likely poor as well as racially oppressed, is a particularly touchy issue for those who view themselves as liberators of the oppressed" (p. 9).

Most researchers who embark on fieldwork in a new setting experience an abundance of anxieties. The biggest fear is whether the members of a community will accept and allow one to probe into their lives for the sake of "scientific knowledge." The type of anxiety experienced, however, depends largely on the community being observed. Communities of older Chicanos have not often been targets of investigation. Thus entry into such a community can be complicated by the subjects' lack of exposure to researchers seeking information about their private and social lives. Such anxieties, for example, can influence decisions and affect dynamics of honesty and consent.

The receptiveness I received was largely based on my ability to speak Spanish and my interest in their lives as elderly women. Generally, older Chicanos are disappointed in younger Chicanos who fail to become bilingual. Many feel that either younger people are ashamed to speak Spanish or parents are irresponsible for failing to teach their children the language. Older Chicanos tend to have a tremendous amount of respect for those in the younger generation who are bilingual. Bilingualism for many older Chicanos is an indication of cultural pride.

It is important to note that in the participant observer phase of the research, my age and sex largely contributed to my building rapport. With respect to age, I was initially referred to as *la señorita,* meaning young single woman. Once they knew I was married, I was recognized by my name, and then eventually affectionately referred to as *mi'ja* or *hija,* meaning "my daughter" or simply "daughter." Both terms also imply an age distinction. In essence, I was affectionately recognized as a young married woman, their surrogate daughter or granddaughter, and not a caseworker or social welfare agent.

The underlying dynamic of my communication with the women was one of a traditional age hierarchy. As a younger person, I was expected to recognize this age hierarchy in granting them respect in my behavior and conversation. For example, I addressed all the women as *señora,* and I deferred to their authority based simply on age. They, too, recognized this hierarchy in acting as educators. This behavior was not always consistent, but it was strongly established as a tradition in the Center.

Related to the age issue were the gender dynamics that took place. The gender tradition established in the Center influenced not only my behavior but my interactions as well. My interactions were limited to the women. With respect to the men, both gender and age influenced my lack of interaction with them. Given that they were elders, I was expected to greet them, but simply out of respect, as a younger person. I did not have extensive conversations with them. In other words, the age dynamic allowed me to greet the men, but gender limited the types of conversations between us. On several occasions when I did attempt to "challenge tradition," the women expressed their disapproval. When I (naively) asked the women to explain their disapproval, they gave two reasons. First, they stated that if a woman approaches a man, her intentions are not considered to be good. Second, they felt that friendships between women and men are all right for younger people, but not for their generation. In other words, these women still operated within very traditional frameworks of male-female relationships.

The process of collecting life histories can be exciting, emotional, and frustrating, as well as time consuming. My explanations of why I was conducting research and for whom did not initially sit well with the women I eventually interviewed. Many were extremely suspicious of my interest in their life histories. The average educational level of these women was roughly 3 years. It was difficult for them to understand the significance of dissertation research. With the exception of one or two women, they had no idea of what dissertation research even meant, and I knew before I asked for their participation that I would have some difficulty. I do not mean to imply that they had no respect for education, because many of their own children were highly educated. However, much like people in the general population, they had little understanding about doctoral programs.

Therefore, the first woman I asked to grant me an interview was the crochet teacher, a woman who was well-respected and had a definite status in the Center. My strategy, needless to say, was to establish accessibility to other women by having the crochet teacher condone their granting interviews. Gradually, other women agreed to be interviewed without any hesitation. Participation increased for several reasons. First, a well-respected Center member provided approval for my work and validation of my intentions by agreeing to be interviewed. Second, as interviews were being collected, some women came to feel that their life histories were worth sharing. Others felt they could educate me about old age. Yet others used the interview as a way of establishing a personal friendship. Some may have agreed to grant interviews for all these reasons. How each woman felt about being interviewed definitely influenced the tone and content of the interview itself.

Of the 30 women selected, 28 were similar to much of the older Chicano population: They immigrated with their families as infants or as young children between 1920 and 1930. The remaining 2 women were born in the United States, in central Texas and in southern California.

Chicanas constitute about 65% of the aged Chicano community. This is not unusual; most aged communities are overwhelmingly composed of women (U.S. Bureau of the Census, 1991). With respect to income, the average household income (1989) was $420 per month. All but three of the women lived alone in either low-income housing, senior citizen housing in low-income areas, or homes that they acquired some 30 to 40 years earlier. One woman lived with her daughter's family, and the other two were married. The average number of years of schooling was 3. The average age of the older Chicanas studied was 71.

My methodological approach in this book, therefore, is ethnographic. Because of my commitment to rediscovering voices and the existence of a rich oral tradition characteristic of Chicano culture, 30 oral histories were collected. In addition, during my 2-year tenure in the field, I acted as a participant observer. These methods were selected based on cultural communication patterns and the accessibility to in-depth information that these techniques make available to the researcher.

The words of older Chicanas are used to convey the meanings of their actions in socially constructing their old age. I attempted to understand the lives of older women based on their own personal reflections, by listening to the voices of these women. Rather than concentrating on one dimension of their lives, I attempted to understand the complexity of being an older Chicana.

As stated by Elsasser et al. (1980), "life histories offer an opportunity to learn from people whose experiences have been eclipsed in standard history books" (p. xviii). The authors argue that in compiling life histories, our concept of social change is broadened. Learning about their determination to define their old age implies that social change also occurs through actions that are individual, private, and often very quiet. Life histories can lead to an appreciation of the ways in which everyday actions may contribute to the shaping of the larger society. The voices of these women tell us that the experiences of older Chicanas—women who have often been stereotyped—are, in fact, richly diverse. The voices spoken here record only a part of the experiences of older Chicanas, but by speaking, "they have transformed their experiences into history" (Elsasser et al., 1980, p. xv). The following are their stories, stories of a generation of women who inform us about being old, poor women of Mexican descent in today's society.

NOTES

1. Torres-Gil (1992) categorized the history of aging in America into three periods: pre-1930 (Young Aging), 1930-1990 (Modern Aging), and post-1990 (New Aging).

2. See Maldonado, 1975. Maldonado argues that social change is breaking down the supportive quality of the traditional family structure. Also see Wallace and Facio, 1987.

3. Cubans represent the wealthiest and most educated Latino group, and have the largest proportion of foreign-born elderly among the three major Latino groups. The largest populations of Puerto Ricans and Cubans are in New York City, New Jersey, and Florida. However, the three states with the largest Latino populations are California, Texas, and Florida (U.S. Bureau of the Census, 1991).

4. These disproportionate ratios result from differences in life expectancy between women and men. At age 65, women can expect to live about 19 more years, compared with 15 more years for men at the same age. At age 75, the comparable figures are 12 more years for women and 9 more years for men. Even at age 85, the life expectancy for females is 1.5 years more than that for males (National Center for Health Statistics, 1990).

5. Research on Chicano aging has focused primarily on the interrelationship of aging and the concept of familism. This approach has been widely accepted and is a primary guiding framework in Chicano aging studies. With few exceptions, Chicano aging research is grounded in an analysis of families as the driving force behind the relationship of the elderly to the larger society. Also, research guided by this concept assumes that most elderly are active primarily within a family context.

6. Accessibility of a potential sample leads to a researcher's making valid judgment choices. I would argue that a criticism of bias in selecting a sample cannot be directed at those researchers studying individuals or groups who are not available in traditional settings for research investigation or toward those individuals conducting ethnographic studies.

2

Entering the World of
Older Chicanos/Mexicans

My entrance to the world of older Chicanos/Mexicans was through a
senior citizen center. My work took me to a social world of later life that
I thought, because of my ethnic and cultural upbringing, would be familiar and comfortable. Much to my surprise, this did not turn out to be the
case. I have always had some type of close contact with older people
through my own grandparents and my *mama Cuca.* My maternal grand-
father had been very close to our family. I cannot remember a time when
abuelito, as my brother called him, lived more than 5 miles from our
home. My paternal grandmother continued to visit regularly during the
winter months. As she advanced in age, the cold winters in Washington
were harder to withstand. Mama Cuca, my "nana," shared hours of conversation with me about her children, her marriage, her life in general,
and the neighborhood where we lived.

I was very anxious about my fieldwork at a senior citizens center that
served Chicano/Mexican elderly and about my intentions to study their
lives. Given my youth, I was unsure how the elderly would respond to
me. Also, my cultural upbringing stressed respect for the aged. Consequently, I did not want to be disrespectful in my behavior. Fortunately,
the Center director, a Chicana herself, was invaluable as both a mediator
and resource person. She shared her concerns about the stigma associated
with the elderly and about the limited amount of research specifically
regarding the Chicano/Mexican aged. The director's support and permission to proceed with my work alleviated my initial anxieties and instilled
a level of confidence and eagerness.

THE CENTER

The Center had operated for about 8 years in one of the city's barrios, a predominantly Chicano/Mexican neighborhood. The Center was funded primarily to provide nutritional and transportation services for the elderly. It was surrounded by railroad tracks and worn Victorian homes reminiscent of the early 1900s. The building was painted with murals symbolically reflecting Chicano/Mexican culture and the historical experiences of the community. The enigmatic character of the Center lured those passing by to glance quickly through the double glass doors.

The Center provided members with noon meals and transportation to and from the Center and occasionally for medical appointments. Other activities such as crafts, local trips, and excursions to Lake Tahoe and Reno were not monetarily supported. Consequently, the seniors had to pay to participate in these activities. The nutrition program provided noon meals for $.50.

Inside, the Center resembled a small school auditorium with a kitchen, portable stage, and partitioned office spaces. The walls were filled with posters written in Spanish and English, discussing health issues such as high blood pressure, heart disease, and a nutritional diet. As one entered, there was a warning that "intoxicated individuals" would be taken home. Small multicolored Mexican rugs decorated the walls. In the back of the Center, a wall-length mural depicted Chicano/Mexican culture. The bright colors of red, orange, yellow, blue, and green, characteristic of Mexican/Chicano art, gave the mural a powerful and aesthetically pleasing presence. The mural was more than just decor; it symbolically constituted images of members as survivors and as sources of ethnic identity such as language, culture, religion, and most important, a common history.

My first day of fieldwork took place during a monthly birthday celebration. On the first Friday of every month, birthdays are celebrated with a dance. On that particular day, banners decorated the walls, spelling *Feliz Cumpleaños*. The enticing aroma of beans, rice, and *carne de res* (shredded beef) filled the air. Three senior male members who make up the Center's band were set up on the small portable stage, playing *rancheras, cumbias,* and *boleros,* songs that have held their popularity for more than 50 years. The music was very familiar. These were songs my family had taught me to appreciate and spiritually embrace.

Nearly 100 seniors attended the birthday celebration, with women outnumbering the men. These aged Chicanos/Mexicanos were obviously no longer employed in the paid labor force. They were advancing in age and appeared to be accepting that fact. The seniors ranged in ages from the mid-60s to the late-70s. There was an evident sense of community among them as older Chicanos/Mexicanos.

Many of the seniors were dressed in what they considered their finest clothing. The clothing and jewelry they proudly wore indicated their class status. Their clothes were obviously not purchased at expensive department stores, and much of their jewelry was inexpensive costume jewelry. Some did bring out jewelry from past years, which now hung very heavy and was somewhat dull. The array of mixed patterns, colors, and costume jewelry in no way affected the image they projected of strong, solid, and proud individuals.

Feeling hesitant and apprehensive, I sat at the end of a table closest to the door, officially beginning my observations while trying to remain anonymous. Within minutes, my youthful appearance provoked baffled, curious glances, mumbling, and many questions. The woman seated next to me, Elena, turned toward me and smiled, making me feel a little less nervous. Elena began asking me questions in Spanish. My ability to converse with her in Spanish facilitated my entrance and subsequent acceptance into the community during the course of my fieldwork.

ELENA: Are you a visitor or are you related to someone here?
EF: Well no . . . yes, I'm visiting for the day. I'm going to be working as a volunteer.

Elena then repeated what I had stated to the women sitting across from her, who immediately struck up a conversation about my life. I, of course, was more than willing to answer any of their questions, in order to establish rapport and use the anthropological approach of communicating to develop a sense of trust.

ELENA: So you're a student, that's good.

At that point, another woman sitting across from me interjected.

TERESA: Where are you from?
EF: From the neighborhood, just a couple of miles from here.
ELENA: Are you married?
EF: Yes, I've been married for 5 years.

The question about marriage caught me totally by surprise. The directness of their questions was a way of learning as much about me as possible. Thus, they went beyond being simply polite. Most likely, they were unsure, doubtful, and suspicious about my sincerity toward them. However, I later learned they were appreciative that someone from my generation was genuinely interested in their lives. The questions continued about my marriage, children, and present residence. I was somewhat unprepared to answer so many questions and was hesitant because I realized that the first few words would be crucial as they would set the stage or define the parameters of my acceptance into this community. After my brief interview, I felt somewhat at ease, able to observe and to interact with the elderly.

The first couple to dance was Angela and Rosa. It is not uncommon for Chicano/Latino women to dance together in public. This behavior is generally not scrutinized among the community and is acceptable, especially among rural populations and the working class. Angela, a 77-year-old widow, has striking green eyes and short silver hair. She was wearing light gray pants and a matching floral blouse, along with peach-colored lipstick. Like many of the women in the Center, she is short. In our private conversations, she would complain about her "wide hips and heavy legs." Rosa, a remarkable 82-year-old, also a widow, was wearing a dark-colored floral dress, stockings, and matching heels. She wore her hair short and dyed auburn red to camouflage her age. Rosa is similar in height to Anna but very slender. She wore thick black glasses and had applied bright rose blush to her warm, wrinkled face. The initiative that women took during dances was an indicator of their high level of activity within the Center. Their actions showed these women to be confident and secure individuals.

There was also a 48th wedding anniversary being celebrated. This definitely was Sra. Martinez's day. She enjoyed all the attention she was receiving, whereas Sr. Martinez remained in the background watching his wife being showered with flowers, embraces, and kisses. I congratulated Sr. Martinez as his wife was promenaded around the room. In reminiscing about his matrimonial years, he mumbled that marriage was very difficult, but the question of divorce was unheard of because "divorce is bad for the children." Meanwhile, Sra. Martinez promenaded around the Center.

Given the festive ambience of the birthday celebration, I assumed the following week would be dreary, marked with depression on the faces of the elderly. However, for older people, every moment seems to be significant. As I spent more time at the Center, I came to the conclusion that there appears to be little time for deception or romanticizing. Patterns of interaction among the Center's members began to take on a particular character. The Center's complexity, structure, and dynamics were being illuminated through my observations.

For example, women would sit together in groups in the back of the Center or along the walls. This simple act, although not necessarily a major dynamic in the Center's operations, is based on territorial rights of individuals segmented by gender, and to some extent conversational topic or interest. In one group, the conversation was about whether Esperanza should be invited to sit with a certain group of women. Vilma sternly stated that she should not be asked because "she made 'bad' faces at me." The actual words Vilma used, *mala cara,* do literally translate to bad or mean face. The popular English cliché, "dirty looks," is a more appropriate translation. Maria, the devout Catholic, gave a religious justification for asking Esperanza to join the others by calmly and convincingly stating, "as a Catholic, it is not right to be judgmental of people." Vilma responded by arguing that Catholicism "says no such thing and has nothing to do with it." A heated argument continued until Vilma went to another table. Maria simply ended the conversation by telling Vilma not to be angry because it was bad for the heart. (Pointing out that anger leads to elevated blood pressures and the danger of heart strain always seemed to end discussions.) The content of the argument appeared trivial and somewhat confusing, as did another I overheard.

TOMAS: I wonder why Mexicans eat fish on Fridays? Every Friday, they [the Center] give us fish.

SARAH: Well, that's the way it has always been, it's a custom.

JOSE: We eat fish on Fridays because the Spaniards brought that religious custom over to Mexico.

TOMAS: But why do we eat fish on Fridays?

SARAH: Because the priests have told us for years, and that's the way it is.

JOSE: Oh, I told you, don't you listen? Those Spaniards taught the Indians that custom!

TOMAS: Yes, but why fish and not chicken?

At that moment, Jose's face turned very red. Quite disgusted, he swore at Tomas under his breath.

Center life, at times, can be passionate, even somewhat melodramatic. In her study of elderly Jews, Barbara Myerhoff (1978) said that inside the environment of a senior citizen center, "ordinary concerns and mundane interchanges are strongly intense, quickly raising to outbursts" (p. 107). The emotional urgency of a conversation many times has little to do with content.

In the third week of my observations, I realized the tremendous amount of time and energy it took to "work my way" into their favor. On many occasions, I would spend the entire afternoon talking with just one person. I attempted to participate in almost every Center activity. On one occasion, the Center had arranged a trip to a railroad museum. I noticed that many of the seniors had dressed up for the occasion. They were all very excited, as many had not been to a museum in years or never before.

I began the tour with Vidal, a slender, short man, who walked with his back slightly hunched, his thin silver hair combed back. Vidal is nearly blind, making it very difficult for him to get around on his own. He is very well liked by all the Center members. While on the tour, we had to sit down occasionally because his legs would begin to ache. He told me he had worked for the railroad for 63 years.

Interestingly, the tour guide himself was an older person. It appeared that the guide had taken this opportunity to show his peers that his memory, speech, and general motor skills were still intact. The group seemed impatient with all the details. However, it was not so much impatience as the fact that the seniors did not understand the English-speaking guide. Many informally broke into small groups and began their own individual tours.

I casually went from group to group, helping them board the trains while listening to their reconstructions of the past. The trip provided a time for reminiscence and storytelling for those who worked on or rode these trains daily. In listening to their narratives, my own preconceived notions of what *old* meant for this community began to be challenged.

Excursions to museums or to Lake Tahoe or Reno had both negative and positive impacts on the aged. Those who were unable to walk long distances or stand for some period of time were functionally categorized as *viejita* or *viejito* (old);[1] this form of labeling was a negative reflection of their aging state. For those seniors who were functionally able to participate in field trips, categorization based on physical abilities served to confirm a healthy and independent status. Thus, functional definitions of age not only enabled the elderly to assess their respective health statuses but were constant reminders of the inevitability and unpredictability of the aging process.

The Center, however, was a place where an individual could be old. It provided emotional support for those who were labeled accordingly. As members supported one another, friendships were solidified. The Center also affirmed many assumptions about the individual's aging state. Many could compare themselves with one another on a physical level and a mental one, to some extent. In some sense, the inevitability of death could be successfully challenged daily by continuing to attend the Center and seeing the same friends. The aged were genuinely concerned with being able to care for themselves, being aware of their personal conditions, and taking responsibility for themselves.

This became particularly clear during monthly blood pressure taking and recording. The Center was responsible for recording blood pressures of all Center members and advising them about diets they should maintain. The Center also provided pamphlets in both Spanish and English listing proper foods for a healthy diet.

Blood pressure checks were one responsibility for the Center's staff that required them to engage in much convincing and persuasion of the senior members. The elderly gave a number of reasons, more likely excuses, for avoiding the process. Many said they did not believe in doctors or in the methods of modern medicine. Others claimed they had already checked with their physicians and that their blood pressure was fine. Then there were those who wore clothing, such as long-sleeved sweaters, making it difficult to record blood pressures.

The ritual of blood pressure taking required people to stand patiently in line and to enter one of the partitioned office areas individually. One could see the obvious anxiety on their faces as their blood pressures were taken. However, the Center director was quite comforting, sensitive, and very personable in telling them about their results.

Those who "passed" the test were quite relieved and boasted of their healthy status. They immediately became experts on proper eating habits. Manuela, in particular, suddenly became rejuvenated, walking throughout the Center with an air of confidence. She began to talk about how salt was one of the most dangerous foods to consume, and how she succeeded in avoiding its use. Manuela's display generated anxiety among several seniors. Sara had returned to request pamphlets on proper diets. She asked if eating certain foods could lead to high blood pressure. I responded by informing her that certain foods were not advisable if one has high blood pressure or any heart problems. She immediately asked me if she was going to die. Sara recited Manuela's sermon on the dangers of using salt. At first, I thought her question was simply rhetorical, but she was very serious. I sat down with her and explained that she appeared to be fine, with normal blood pressure. I then told her that as long as her blood pressure was low, there was not any immediate danger; I suggested that she consult the Center nurse as well as her personal doctor. Feeling comfortable and somewhat convinced by my response, she thanked me and joined the others in conversations regarding their health.

Whereas some left the area relieved and somewhat proud, others left feeling quiet, disappointed, and fearful of the unpredictability of time. In such situations, the Center was a place where people could elicit emotional support and sympathy, even though they risked the possibility of being singled out and negatively categorized. Regardless of the severity of their health problems, the aged did not conceal their daily aches and pains. Their enlisting of empathetic attention was almost exaggerated at times. Nonetheless, the empathetic character of this attention was what appealed to the elderly. The Center is unique in providing empathetic support; individuals outside the Center are more likely to pity the aged or to consider their recurring health problems a nuisance.

The Center allowed the aged to accept the unpredictable and inevitable nature of the aging process. Celebrating life during monthly birthday parties was a triumph of survival. This was evident in remarks made by Marequita, the Center president, during birthday celebrations. As she introduced all those celebrating a birthday, Marequita would relate anecdotes of a particular achievement, whether it was related to their health, their children, their grandchildren, or their own accomplishments. She would reflect on their past struggles and present lives. This part of her speech always generated a round of applause. She finally ended by acknowledging and giving thanks to God.

INTERACTION OF AGE AND GENDER: SELF-WORTH AND CONTINUITY

After a few weeks of observation and informal discussions with the elderly, I began to detect the Center's structure, dynamics, and complexity. Within the Center, women had created certain groups that were gender-specific, concerned with what is generally considered "women's work."

One group, *Las Abuelas* (The Grandmothers), was religious in character. Members were mainly involved with Catholic church activities associated with religious and cultural holidays. Occasionally, the local Catholic church would call on Las Abuelas to assist in local fund raisers. For example, they would prepare *tamales* or *menudo* for cultural events such as Cinco de Mayo or the 16th of September. There were roughly 12 members, Maria, Josefina, and Lupe being the most active and outspoken.

Maria, a widow who lived alone, was 73 and the mother of seven children. Maria projected a very strong and stern character. Her body was stocky. She walked with confidence, head held up high. Maria wore her hair in a hair net. It reminded me of the way women who work in canneries wear their hair, like my mother. Of all the Abuelas, she was most proud of her knowledge of Catholicism. Josefina was probably the most active member of this group. At 77, she had tremendous spirit, was compassionate and very confident. She highly valued education and was thankful for the good relationships she had with her three sons. Lupe, also a widow, was 84; she appeared frail and somewhat vulnerable. Lupe would greet the other women with prolonged embraces, as though she was seeking acceptance, attention, a sense of being needed. She required reassurance about her individual self worth. Compared with Maria and Josefina, she had only her membership in the group to call attention to her presence.

Las Abuelas played a large part in involving other seniors to participate in church-affiliated events. For example, a cultural celebration that remains significant for this group is *Dia de los Muertos* (All Souls Day), celebrated on November 2 to honor and remember deceased relatives. On that particular day, a sign-up sheet was passed around the Center to those seniors interested in participating in a procession organized by this group. We were scheduled to meet in the early evening at a local high school about a mile from the cemetery, and we were instructed to walk there with lit candles. The number of individuals who participated was small; as in most activities, women outnumbered men. Those men who did attend were informally recognized with overeffusive embraces as if the women had not seen these men in some time, even though they had been together several hours earlier at the Center. The warm and prolonged greetings verified unity among a group of individuals who are isolated from and peripheral to the dominant society. Their joining together as a group legitimized not only their presence but the significance of their culture. Only outside the Center, where security is uncertain, does such behavior tend to occur. A young man in his teens, dressed in a long dark serape with black pants, or what are referred to as "khakis," guided the procession. He carried a wooden cross about 2 to 3 feet tall with a papier-mâché skeleton symbolizing that homage would be paid to deceased members of the Chicano/Mexican community. The seniors followed closely behind, many dressed in black with rosaries in their hands, singing Mexican traditional songs of the past. As we arrived at one of the altars, a priest was present to conduct a short ceremony, while the seniors filled the altar with gifts of pictures, liquor, soda, beans, candles, and Mexican sweet bread.

The next day, I took my tape recorder to the Center to ask Las Abuelas more about Dia de los Muertos. The importance of this celebration for these women is in being able to maintain a spiritual bond with deceased relatives.

> JOSEFINA: What we did in Mexico during this celebration is that we went to the cemetery taking flowers, candles, and we prayed. There is a bread called "bread of the deceased." We used to buy it outside the cemetery, and eat it on that day to make sure that we were all there as one. And we do this because we believe it is a way of being spiritually close to the deceased.
>
> MARIA: We have this responsibility to all our past relatives. I am devoted to pray each day during the month of November for my husband who died 15 years ago. I also pray for my parents who are buried in Mexico. This is a tradition that we learned from our grandmothers and mothers.

Las Abuelas also were confronted with fears associated with death and subsequently with their own mortality. For these women, participating in such activities provides a means to deal with the inevitable occurrence of death.

A second group, the Crochet Club, was organized by Gloria, a 71-year-old widow. Gloria lived alone in a home she and her husband had purchased some 40 years ago. Gloria suffered a stroke nearly a year before I met her. In our private conversations, she told me that she was determined to be as independent as possible. She used a cane when she walked but still fell occasionally. However, she has not allowed her disability to hinder her or dampen her spirits. An extremely handsome woman with curly salt-and-pepper hair and a fabulous smile, Gloria would dance and sing along with the Mexican music that played throughout the Center, even though she could not carry a tune.

The Crochet Club gathered almost every day to receive instructions on how to improve their crocheting techniques and how best to complete a particular item. More important, strategies for selling their products were discussed. Gloria customarily seated herself at the center of a table giving instructions while overseeing the women working on their projects. The women crocheted anything from potholders to afghans. The best moneymakers were vests, *chalecos,* infant clothing such as sweaters with matching hats and booties, and baby blankets. The most popular items were christening outfits. When asked why she organized this group, Gloria replied,

> I used to work in the canneries. In the off-season, I would work at the sanitarium for tuberculosis patients. I used to clean and help the people walk around, things like that. They assigned me to work with women. That's when I learned to crochet. I would crochet scarves, hats, and sell them to the patients. When they would ask me to make something, I would tell them that they would have to pay me first. Then I started bringing in jalapeño peppers and sold them, too, because they liked them. When the hospital closed down, I kept crocheting things and sold them and worked in the canneries. That's how I've made a living. I'm not saying I'm good, but I started classes here with the other ladies. This way they have something to do and can make a little bit of money.

Two members of this group, Nieves and Amelia, regularly sat together at the end of the table, observing and listening to Gloria. From their behavior, I assumed they were new group members. They appeared to be very content. Both wore their long gray hair up in braided buns with scarves. Both wore glasses and a sweater over large baggy dresses, similar orthopedic shoes, and support hose. The warm, friendly faces of these women were facades covering a fear of appearing ignorant to other members of the group or other seniors in the Center. Projecting such an assured image never really allowed anyone to probe them. At times, I had difficulty making conversation with them, not because they were unfriendly, but because their dispositions did not allow me to overstep any boundaries.

Participation in the center's activities allowed Nieves and Amelia to be seen and honored, to become visible and receive attention. The knowledgeable and confident image helped to establish a positive self-worth, something they would not easily obtain in the outside world.

Trini and Patricia, on the contrary, responded differently to my presence. At times, I sensed they were "performing" for me. They appeared to know exactly what they were doing. When I came around to sit and observe their work, they became much more efficient. I was not sure whether I was projecting myself as a supervisor or as an interested person, so I asked them about their work and complimented them as well. When they asked me if I knew how to crochet, I told them that it looked too difficult. This gave them the opportunity in a sense to "compete with me on equal ground." Through the knowledge of crocheting, they were able to establish a sense of power.

This struggle of power relations between young and old often surfaced. I, the younger person, symbolically reflected youth, an oppressive constituent of society to the old. Thus, Center members attempted to refute stereotyped notions of the elderly as inadequate, nonproductive individuals. Their efficient crocheting provided an opportunity to display their creative abilities. It was also a means to call themselves to the attention of someone from the outside world.

A third and final group included Center Volunteers. These individuals were responsible for maintaining the Center and setting tables for the noon meals. Their tasks included putting out tablecloths, condiments, and beverages, and serving lunches in an assembly line fashion. These volunteers consisted of only women. They arrived as early as 8:30 a.m. to begin their tasks, which required anywhere from 2 to 3 hours of preparation. In return, the volunteers were entitled to free meals. Esperanza, Ana, Antioñia, and Marequita were distinguished from the others by their rose-colored aprons with "volunteer" written across the front.

Marequita was mainly in charge of serving coffee. She stood off to one side of the serving line with the coffee machine, which was placed on a small table. I spent a lot of time with her, as she had been a member since the Center opened. Marequita's physical movements were slow and cautious, making her appear somewhat passive. With each cup of coffee that she filled, I was informed about the Center and its members.

I volunteer because I need something to do with my time and I get free meals, saves me a little bit of money. I don't want to be like some of these people, they take whatever they can. A lot of them take the salsa on the tables. They bring jars and use their milk cartons and slip them into their bags. Las Abuelas were making a beautiful afghan for the church, the

church paid them to do it, but I think somebody in here stole it. But that's
life and I still like to come here. We dance, sing, and I like the birthday
celebrations.

I continued to probe her about differences in behavior among women and
men. More specifically, I was interested in knowing if aging for women
was distinctly different from the experiences of men. She replied,

You know, the men are so lazy, they don't even pick up the cup where they
drink their coffee, my goodness! The other day an old man said, "where do
you live?" I said, "in my house," then he asked me, "can I come and visit
you?" I said, "no, I have my boyfriend." [At that point, she giggled and
blushed.] I said, "no visitors allowed!" There's a lot of women here who
like those old men, but they don't tell them. But me, I'm not afraid to tell a
man I like him. . . . But, the men and women are different here at the
Center. The men look like they're lost, they're very quiet. Life is hard for
all of us, we're poor, a lot of us are sick, we get arthritis. We're just waiting,
but here at the Center, we can wait together. We just thank God that He
brings us here everyday.

Waiting, as Marequita explained, is not a deliberate, conscious act, but
the elderly are obviously aware of their advanced age and that time is
both limited and unpredictable.

The groups generated opportunities to be seen, respected, and honored, a way of to get visibility and attention. The elderly in general seek
to establish a sense of self-worth vis-à-vis each other. The aged, according to Myerhoff (1978), "are basically regarded as an oppressive group
whose lives are largely determined by forces beyond their control, engen-
dering a preoccupation with honor and self-worth" (p. 39). Without natu-
ral audiences to witness their lives, Center members were considered
obsolete in the outside world. Hence, activities and group organizations
were markers of existence and a display of worth. Chicano elderly
women have constructed Center life as a world that serves as a frame
within which people can appear, be seen, act, interact, and exist.

Overall, women as a group appeared more complex, active, and confident. Men, on the contrary, were quieter, more vague, seemingly more
obsolete than women. Myerhoff (1978) suggested that in social structures such as a senior citizen center, men find themselves primarily preoccupied in finding a new balance of involvement with themselves and
other members. Among the women, the underlying dynamic of participa-

tion is largely reflective of both family structures and prior occupational experiences characteristic of a distinct sexual division of labor by gender. Las Abuelas, for example, accommodating to the institutions and regulations set forth by men, continue their role as facilitators of religion. Preservation of Catholicism, by teaching prayers and by participating in rituals such as baptism, communion, and confirmation, was a duty taught to these women during childhood through the example of their mothers and/or grandmothers.

Center activities such as crocheting, preparation of meals, and maintenance of the Center involve patterns of domesticity that have been extended from both the home and labor market and are now performed within the Center.

This particular differentiation of old age among the Center's aged is partially inherent in the system of patriarchy. Hartmann (1979) suggested that the operation of this principle has historically relegated women to the "private" sphere, the domestic domain where household maintenance, child care, nurturance, interpersonal relationships, and the creation of an emotional ambience of the home take place. In contrast, men assume responsibility for the "public" sphere, the world of work, providing for the family's economic subsistence. Distinctions between public and private domains remain prevalent during the aging process for this particular generation of aged Chicanos/Mexicanos.

However, we must question what enables older Chicanas to maintain a distinct sense of continuity in the aging process. One plausible explanation may be that during old age, social roles allocated to the elderly are predominantly associated with the private sphere. As Myerhoff (1978) pointed out, "retired people in society, both men and women, are expected to spend their time socializing, taking care of themselves, passing the days pleasantly, attending to the quality of life and interpersonal concern" (p. 262). With the loss of work, men in general lose their link to the dimension of the public sphere. This not only costs the retired man his ability to earn money but also impairs his sense of self-worth and autonomy. Men are expected to devote themselves, after retirement, to areas in which they have little prior experience, areas they were often taught to regard as demeaning.

Accordingly, women have an advantage over men inasmuch as their primary responsibilities associated with the private domain continue to be viable in the later years. As illustrated by Center activities, older Chicanas used skills of the private sphere that have been historically prescribed by gender.

Thus, old age may call for an expansion of the tasks characteristic of the private sphere, allowing aged Chicanas to exert a strong sense of vitality, dominance, and power. Through the creation of Center groups and activities, Chicana/Mexicana elderly were able to display their abilities in establishing interpersonal relationships, being able to care for themselves as well as others. The principle of patriarchy, however, is not exclusive to the domestic domain. As mentioned earlier, Chicana/Mexican women have historically been concentrated in low-paying jobs determined by the interplay of class, race/ethnicity, and gender. Thus, during old age, Chicanas find themselves poorer than men and challenged in developing supplemental means of economic subsistence. The selling of crafts and crocheting products supplements monthly incomes. Providing their services as Center volunteers in exchange for free meals constitutes a means of labor. With each meal at a cost of $.50 a day, or $10 a month, they save a substantial amount of money. Household production, formerly performed by women within the home and in the informal service sector, has been shifted to sites such as the Center, which has extended their wage-earning capacities.

RELOCATION OF THE CENTER

During the 2-year period when this research took place, the Center was relocated just several blocks from its original site. An expired rental lease and rent increases forced the move. Although state, law, real estate, and physicians' offices are now settled in the area, the Center's old building remains painted with murals, symbolically reflecting Chicano/Mexican culture and the historical experiences of the community.

The Center, now situated in a high-crime section of the neighborhood, is located within a Neighborhood Center where different social programs are offered to the community. Information and referral services such as jobs (e.g., summer youth programs), educational services, legal advice, and monthly food rations were provided.

On my daily drives to the new Center, I first noticed the change in the homes as I entered the neighborhood. They were older, run-down, yet beautifully constructed Victorian homes. The local bar on the corner was a marker of entry into the neighborhood. The bar was well-known for its weekend fighting and occasional killings. Slow signs of gentrification had made their way into this section of the neighborhood, as well: The occasional law or real estate office in a renovated Victorian, freshly painted with handcrafted signs in English (so as not to appear too far removed from the community), Audis and BMWs securely parked, seemed to be misplaced among the local "mom-and-pop" store on the corner and the social service program for ex-convicts. Chicano/Mexican men of various ages were drinking as early as 10:00 a.m. and obviously claimed the corner of 3rd and Mariposa street. Older men, primarily Chicanos/Mexicanos, pushing all of their belongings in shopping carts, greeted many of the seniors on their way to the Center. Others were unemployed, recently arrived immigrants. Toward the edge of the neighborhood were "the projects," a prevalent feature of many Chicano barrios. Drugs and gangs plagued the neighborhood. Many people, however, struggled to clean it up. In the midst of all this were the tall buildings of food-processing plants, one of the major industries of this city, which towered over the neighborhood, filling the air with loud noises and the aromas of fruits and vegetables.

The new Center was much smaller and did not have the same atmosphere as the other. The faded yellow walls filled with bilingual posters about health issues, the symbolic decor of Mexican flags, small multicolored Mexican rugs, and the wall-length mural depicting Chicano/Mexican culture—all were gone.

But despite the Center's dismal location and appearance, it was a place of extraordinary significance for those who gathered there daily.

The Center is a place with a lot of spirit, it's so beautiful with all the women crocheting and Victorio playing the guitar. It's a very important place, we need that kind of environment in our lives. . . . The Center is for the poor people, it's not for rich people. Some have come in here and they're not satisfied. All they do is come in and complain, they think they're better than everybody. But we, we like the Center, it's all some of us have. We don't need those kind of people to make us feel like we're nobody.

The existence and recognition of poverty among these elderly was revealed. The Center was a place where Chicano/Mexicano elderly could be open about their hardships and look to others for emotional and social support when needed.

Many times, the elderly criticized the Center and its members, but they did so with restraint. For example, Alicia discussed the directorship and overall condition of the Center in whispers, concluding, "and those things I said to you about the Center, they're not going to come out on the tape? because, no, no, no . . . I'm very happy at the Center." Other comments or criticisms of the Center always began with: "I'm going to tell you something, so don't say anything" or "but I'm telling you in confidence."

These comments are an indication of the significance the Center has for the aged. The seniors in essence were protecting the Center by asking that their comments not be made public. This protectiveness and reluctance to complain stems from their pride in the Center; for many, *they* are the Center. For others, this is the only place they frequent outside their homes. Their reluctance to criticize the Center and the way in which they offered criticisms were strong indications of the importance the Center had in their lives.

For many of those who attend, the Center was a major part of their daily activities. As Concepcíon said,

> I get up every day at 5 in the morning, I have my coffee and start crocheting until about 7:30 or 8. Then I get ready to go to the Center, and I stay there until 3 or 3:30, and I do that every day.

The aged provided a variety of reasons as to why they attended the Center, ranging from being lonely to needing to establish a sense of self-worth and looking for friendship. Generally, all those who attended did so as a way of dealing with loneliness and the desire for social interaction. Lupe summed up these feelings:

> You know, when a person is alone, sometimes you say, "why cook for just myself?" At the Center, I just pay $1 and I have my food. Sometimes I go to restaurants to eat. But a person feels lonely, they need to talk with other people, with people over there (the Center). I need to pass the time talking with other people. There are some that say, "Not me, I'd rather eat at home." Why sure, but people like to go to places like the Center to talk with people, so they won't be so lonely. A person makes friends and they invite you to go shopping. We pass the time real nice.

Others allude to children no longer being in a position to give their aged parents attention. Maria, for example, said, "The Center is the only place I go to. I visit my children, but they all have their separate and busy lives. Sometimes I get in the way, and I don't want to get in their way."

In Cuellar's (1978) study, he described two types of lonely senior citizen club members, the network constructor and companion seeker.

According to Cuellar, "the network constructor uses the voluntary association as a basis for building her or his personal social network" (p. 216). This applies specifically to those individuals whose only social contacts are with members of senior citizen centers.

The companion seeker in Cuellar's study referred to the younger women who attended the voluntary association. This category included women who ranged from 36 to 44 years old. In my study, the youngest woman interviewed was 60. In this case, age does play a factor in how open a person is to companionship.

The second category of responses revolved around individual self-esteem, the need to establish a sound and positive identity among peers at the center. Rosa said, "They give certificates to people who volunteer, you know, help out at the Center. I go every day and they recognize me for that. I've received two certificates." Others, such as Ysidra, gave similar responses:

> I've liked the Center since we were in the other place. I like it because people would tell me, "write some letters to the Council and let them know about us, they're asleep up there." So I used to write letters for the old people, because I know a little bit of English.

Cuellar (1978) also found in his study that voluntary associations serve as a means of generating prestige: "As a public arena for social interaction, the senior citizens club gives older Chicanos the opportunity to demonstrate their competence and ability to learn new roles" (p. 217).

Women like Lucia implied in their responses that they came not only because of feelings of loneliness and the need to establish a positive self-esteem but also because it was important to the creation of friendships. She said,

> I go to the Center because it's too lonely to be in the house by yourself. The Center helps me pass the time away, time passes fast. I've made friends, we talk, crochet. The women have been nice to me. When I go, a lot of them ask me to help them crochet.

Others, such as Antioñia, also refer to the importance of friendship. She said,

> We go to the Center for two reasons, one because we go to talk and we knit, we learn from one another, we learn how to make a certain food, how to

make a cake, and this is how we enjoy and help one another. If I have a lot of tomatoes, I'll take them some. If they have tomatoes or apples, they bring me some.

Friendships among these women are a strong basis of emotional and social support. One can argue that the support they no longer received from their immediate families was taken up by the networks established in the Center. This assumes, however, that the family has and will continue to provide support, regardless of the social and economic conditions facing them. I argue that familial networks are based on obligation, whereas friendship networks operate from a base of equality.

Settling into the new Center was initially difficult. Attendance was lower, activities decreased, people were disappointed with how the Center was being financially directed. Nonetheless, many of the elderly recreated the traditions established in the previous Center.

After the move to the new location, Las Abuelas basically dissolved for financial reasons. This group was funded by a local nonprofit community organization for the work they did for the church. Once the funds had been depleted, this group was no longer as visible as in the former Center. Only a few women actively promoted the importance of religious practices. However, this allowed other women, in particular Señora Rodriguez, to take part in maintaining and recognizing Catholic traditions in the Center.

These women designed a small altar consisting of a small statue of the Virgin de Guadalupe and a picture of El Niño Fidencio placed inside a plain white wooden structure designed like a church with candles, rosaries, and flowers.[2] These women—Sra. Rodriguez, Anita, Sara, and Patricia—were now referred to as the Altar Caretakers. They were recognized for their knowledge of Catholicism and respected for carrying on tradition.

The Crochet Club changed in membership but continued to operate very much the way it had at the previous location. These women ultimately became the most powerful group in the Center because they were able to maintain the group's continuity. Unlike Las Abuelas, they were not dependent on outside monetary resources.

Like the crochet group, Center Volunteers changed in membership but not in structure. Center Volunteers were not primarily women from a group referred to as the socializers. With the move to the new Center location, variations of the previous groups had formed. The important point is not so much whether membership or structure changed but the purpose these groups served.

At the new Center, it was not difficult for these modified groups to establish their presence and pursue tasks of developing a positive self-image and dealing with economic survival. This was due to the fact that previous women's groups had already established a strong tradition. In essence, this tradition was carried over and perpetuated through the modified women's groups. Basically, these new groups were an extension of the previous women's groups associated with the old Center location.

CENTER INTERACTION

The women's groups not only provided a means of establishing a positive self-worth and mechanisms of economic subsistence, but they also generated complex patterns of interaction. The very presence of these groups shaped interaction among members and with the men of the Center. In essence, the formation of the women's groups acted as a symbolic response to a long history of male domination, thus allowing them to deal with these repressed feelings.

Competition, jealousy, gossip, and sexual antagonism cast a shadow on Center interaction. Many times people's interactions were somehow trivial but yet complex and very intense. The previous two examples—the discussions of whether Esperanza should sit with a particular group and why Mexicans eat fish on Fridays are cases in point.

Intense discussions were very much a part of Center interaction. With further observation, I learned that their interactions were more than just trivial. There were more specific reasons why they interacted the way they did. No doubt, the unpredictability of time was a factor. However, as previously mentioned, establishing a positive image among one's peers was extremely important to these individuals. Jealousy, competition, and gossip were crucial factors that influenced interaction among the women. Interaction between women and men was primarily determined or shaped by gender dynamics.

The interaction among the elderly is best understood if we begin with the Center's physical makeup. The Center's structural arrangement was organized, by the women's request, according to gender and the particular activities with which women were involved. Competition further differentiated the organization of the tables. Jealousy existed as a consequence of the competition but did not significantly alter interaction among the women. Gossip served as a mechanism to solidify the boundaries these women had created.

Each table had its own distinct character. One table was assigned to married couples only. Other tables were for men, some of them widowers; others simply there to enjoy the company of other men. The most visible tables were those designated for the three groups of women that I have designated the Crochet Club, the Socializers, and the Altar Caretakers.

Each group had a vested interest in maintaining the established boundaries of interaction. One's identity—whether it was good, bad, right, or wrong—was insignificant. More important was association with a particular group. Each group member was expected to interact accordingly. Any deviation from the group's standards led to open discussions, a public scrutiny by a particular table. These actions were a means of further solidifying the boundaries as well as the particulars of the group.

One incident illustrated the competition among the groups. A woman who was associated with the Socializers tried to become more involved with the Crochet Club. Like many of the other seniors, Carmen customarily greeted everyone in the Center, including the crochet experts. However, on one occasion, she went beyond simply greeting them and began asking them questions about their crocheting. She asked if they were using a particular type of crocheting skill, one with which she was familiar. After she had asked a number of questions, the women began slowly to tune her out. At one point, she ended up talking to herself. She politely dismissed herself and proceeded to her regular table. It appeared she intended to break down boundaries between the two groups, and boundaries between herself and the group, by informing them of her limited knowledge and skills.

Gossip served to solidify the boundaries of each group. Each group accused the other of gossiping. Partaking in gossip and making gross speculations about one another was a conscious activity. Friendships dissolved and disrespect for one another escalated. Such interaction only occurred, however, when a group's structure, form, and composition were threatened.

Competition among the groups became even more apparent when the least powerful and nonthreatening group, the Socializers, associated with the other two groups. As an example, Patricia would sit with the Crochet Club until members of her own group arrived at the Center. Her interaction with the crochet group was very casual. Upon the arrival of her group members, she would politely excuse herself, wish them a good day, and go sit with the Socializers. Patricia's interaction with the crochet experts was not viewed as competition or rudeness; it was simply recognized and accepted that she was not affiliated with these women.

A definite hierarchy existed among the groups. The Crochet Club was the most dominant, followed by the Altar Caretakers, then by the Socializers. Given this hierarchical structure, the interaction between the crochet experts and altar workers, not surprisingly, was often intense. The groups were mechanisms to establish a visible and positive identity; the Center became a place where the members could have positive identities as older people. Outside of this environment, such an identity was very difficult to establish.

Interestingly, the conflicts that stemmed from this hierarchical group structure were rarely made public to the entire Center. In other words, intense interactions were kept within the groups and did not include melodramatic displays of emotion. However, Center members were well-aware of the dynamics. Lucia provided an interesting view of the antagonisms between the groups: "I don't know why we fight—we're old, we're all ugly. [She laughed.] We might be dead before we settle our differences. We're not children, we shouldn't fight."

Behavior of these groups was complex. Despite struggles within and between them, the groups operated collectively in exerting power and establishing control over the Center. This collective behavior was directed at the men who attended the Center, thus establishing a power struggle between the sexes. These conflicts between women and men were made known to the entire Center.

SEXUAL ANTAGONISM

Sexual antagonism between the women and men in the Center was displayed through various activities and interactions. For example, women created specific activities for women only, such as the Christmas Club. The exercise class also became identified as a woman's activity. There was generally a lot of joking and name calling between the women and men. This taunting was all done "in fun." For example, during the exercise classes, some men would say out loud that the women should be home "cleaning house." Men occasionally acknowledged women according to the group with which they were associated. Some women were called "nosy," others "gossipers."

This sexual antagonism became most evident during monthly birthday dances. Dances were customarily opened by a couple comprised of women. It was noted earlier that women dancing with women is an acceptable form of behavior, especially among rural populations and the working class. Further investigation revealed another reason why women danced together: the social relationships that existed between women and men. This was evident in the following conversation I had with several women about the birthday celebrations. One woman began,

> I really like the dances. I never miss the birthday parties. We dance for an hour or two, after we have our meal. We're so happy with life during birthdays, women with women, of course.

Another woman added,

> We don't feel bad about dancing with one another. Why should we? It's beautiful. A dance is a dance. A lot of women have asked me to dance, it doesn't bother me to dance with a woman. On the contrary, they say I'm a good dancer, that's good. I dance with Marequita, Dora, Esperanza, and even Francisca, who's 80 years old. We just enjoy ourselves.

I then asked why women did not dance with the men. One woman boldly responded that they were "lazy."

> They just want to watch the poor old ladies walk back and forth like crazy looking for a dance partner but they don't move because they're lazy. That's why and they don't dance because most of them think they're too good. There are only a few men who really like to dance. The others, they just look at us, but don't ask. But Don Juanito, the short man, he always dances, and he's married. But he doesn't dance with his wife. He dances with everyone else, but he does dance the love songs with her. Tomas and the other short man who sits on the corner, Don Panfilo, dances. But the rest, they don't dance. I think the men see us as being stronger, having more spirit. They're envious. Maybe they don't know how to approach us. They're afraid, I think, to offend us.

The sexual antagonism between the men and women appears to stem from women's pent-up feelings. These women have experienced various forms of male domination. For example, they have been the primary caregivers of the household and children. Their husbands often decided whether or not they worked outside the home. In general, their lives have

been largely directed and determined by their husbands. Their antag-
onistic behavior toward the men was a conscious effort to establish a
sense of independence, a way of protecting themselves from further
vulnerability.

Chicana elderly have consequently created an environment where they
can exercise a sense of independence, power, and control. However, in
this process, the men have become somewhat isolated. Many men have
verbally expressed their resentment toward the women. Sra. Ramirez recalled when one of the men said they no longer cared to attend the Center
because all the women did was gossip. She responded, "Well, if you
don't like it, don't come to the Center. . . . You men argue more than you
talk!" Thus, in the Center, the interaction among the women and men is
limited, casual, and many times tense.

Their interactions, however, also stem from their traditional perspectives about female and male relationships. Thus, two dynamics shape
their interactions: feelings of repression and traditional ideals regarding
male/female relationships. Marta and Virginia referred to these ideas:

> MARTA: Men and women talking as friends is modern, you know, contempo-
> rary. Our (elderly) ideas are very old-fashioned.
>
> VIRGINIA: Look, if one person talks to another, they already have them en-
> gaged!

These traditional ideologies come into conflict with their need to display a sense of independence. On the one hand, these women no longer
cared to tolerate male dominance. They wanted to feel comfortable
enough to associate with men and create friendships on more equal
terms. On the other hand, traditional gender perspectives on male/female
relationships served as a means of control, placing these women in vulnerable positions. Thus, these women felt pressured to act in a gender-
defined context or a respectable manner. For example, Ruth commented
that some women were seeking companionship. She said that such
women were labeled as "flirts," and their behavior was viewed as unac-
ceptable for the Center. Outside the Center was where such behavior
should take place, if at all. Antioñia's comment also reflected this contradiction:

> Well, the reason why we don't talk to one another in that way is because
> people start to talk. They think bad things, they think just because you talk
> to someone that you're interested in them, you see . . . that's why a lot of

women don't talk to the men. . . . Like Ana, you see how she is? . . . Well,
a lot of them (men) might think we're all like her.

The complexity of Center interaction was largely determined by age
and gender dynamics. The interaction between women was primarily
shaped by age. Their need to establish a sense of self-worth was a direct
response to an aging process that no longer grants them a positive identity and a defined status in their immediate families and society at large.
Their responses to this challenge were evident in the activities and interactions they employed to ensure a positive age identity. Continuity of
women's groups stemmed from continuous, active participation in a particular group, thus solidifying its existence. Competition, jealousy, and
gossip were mechanisms of resistance. Such mechanisms were employed
when a group's existence was threatened.

Second, the intense interaction between women and men has resulted
primarily from women's past experiences with male domination.
Women's groups were a symbolic display of their intolerance for further
male control. These groups were an expression of their desire for independence and control in their aging process or over their lives as older
women. In their struggles to establish a sense of control, traditional ideologies of male/female relationships were in direct conflict with their
efforts. Nonetheless, this tension was somewhat resolved. The very existence of women's groups indicated their willingness to construct their old
age.

CENTER LIFE
AS CULTURAL EXPRESSION

Finally, Chicano/Mexican elderly established the Center as an arena of
cultural expression. Physical aspects of culture, such as Mexican food,
Mexican music, and the Spanish language, were maintained in the Center. Outsiders who visited or individuals who worked in the Center were
obligated to respect the playing of Mexican music and particularly the
speaking of Spanish. As an example, two women came from an outside
health agency to speak on Medicaid. Even though they were not fluent in
Spanish, they were expected to communicate with the seniors the best
way they could. Translators were made available when absolutely necessary. Other physical aspects of Chicano culture were also expressed,
such as traditional Mexican celebrations (e.g., Cinco de Mayo, 16th of

September, and All Souls Day or Dia de los Muertos). The actual cultural practices associated with each celebration were also maintained. Finally, two other aspects of Chicano culture were expressed, the traditional age hierarchy and the notion of *respeto* or respect. The traditional age hierarchy applied primarily to outsiders. Those individuals who either visited or worked at the Center were expected to acknowledge this age hierarchy by formally addressing the seniors as *señora, doña, señor,* or *don.* The seniors themselves, however, addressed each other on a first-name basis. Only when seniors were not familiar with one another did they address each other as señora or señor. When speaking of one another in the third person, they also referred to another senior as señora or señor.

The traditional age hierarchy finds less confirmation in everyday life outside the Center than it once did. The ideology of this age hierarchy has remained a strong cultural value. Consequently, Chicano aged maintain this dimension of culture by adhering to traditional interaction and practices of acknowledgment based on age.

Related to the age hierarchy is the notion of respect. The cultural value of respeto for the aged is also an established tradition in the Center. Juanita, for example, said, "Places like the Center can be good for old people. There's a lot of arguing and gossiping, but there's a lot of joy, good friends, and respect of everyone."

In general, the seniors reinforced, maintained, and preserved the traditional value of respect among themselves. The aged in this study said that their immediate families respect them, but the value of respect for the aged finds less confirmation in everyday life beyond the family. Respect appeared to be largely confined to the family and did not extend to the larger community. Each family might state that respect for the aged is a strong cultural value, but this belief was not reflected in the community at large. In other words, respect for the aged was no longer formally, but only informally, recognized and practiced. Respect is an assumed cultural value that has been taken for granted and its realization is now limited to the immediate family structure.

The following comments reflected opinions concerning respect for the aged. Chicano aged in general said that the value of respect is still a strong cultural value, but that its actualization is practically nonexistent.

There are a lot of people here with grandkids who are disrespectful . . . some of them. It used to be different when I was younger, they used to respect you more. Now some of them, to me I think sometimes . . . I'm not going to give them the chance to disrespect me.

Respect is not unconditionally granted, and one must struggle with younger cohorts in order to be respected according to the elderly's ideas of respect.

Whether the young generation respects you or not, depends on the family, how they're raised, so there are some who are real rebellious and there are some that are not.

Respect for the aged is an important cultural value that families must socialize in their children.

It was different before. In my time when I was young, we respected our parents so much that you couldn't say nothing that would disrespect them. I had experiences with my own daughter, she would say, "Mother, you're an old-timer, Mom, you have old-fashioned ideas and it's not that way anymore." I said, "well, the ideas and the habits that we had in my day, they were very good."

Many of the elderly would make similar statements by providing extensive narratives of what was expected of them as children and young adults in their behavior toward the aged. They gave detailed scenarios of how grandparents, aunts, and uncles disciplined children who were disrespectful. Judging by their quotes and narratives, they expected to be treated in old age the way their parents and grandparents were. They were socialized to expect traditional practices of respect, which in turn would provide a secure and defined relationship with their families and the community at large.

In line with Cuellar's (1978) argument, this can be regarded as a major discontinuity or contradiction: Senior citizens centers for Chicano elderly provide a means of responding creatively to the contradictions and discontinuities of old age. This suggests that, for many older members of the Chicano community, traditional arenas of engagement no longer completely respond to their needs.

Cuellar argued that one of the major contradictions the Chicano/ Mexican aged face results from the interaction of two cultures. Although most of the Chicano/Mexican elderly have severed ties with their communities of origin, at the same time, they have not become acculturated into the Anglo society in which they live. Because of this, they have lost a way of maintaining continuity with their children and grandchildren, who are generally more acculturated than themselves (Becerra, 1983; Cuellar, 1978).

Senior citizen centers provide a way to mitigate at least some of the negative losses and discontinuities experienced in aging and to maintain some of the positive continuities associated with old age in the Chicano/ Mexican community. With respect to positive continuities, this argument proposes that Chicano/Mexican aged are able to turn to one another to structure their old age in the content of senior citizen centers where continuity can be maintained through the preservation of ethnicity. In establishing the Center as an arena of cultural expression, the elderly have persistently and creatively responded to this contradiction or discontinuity.

However, on one level, respeto serves as a strong mechanism of control. The notion is proposed in the literature as strictly culturally based. However, some of its features are well-rooted in dimensions of control and subordination associated with age and gender. No doubt, the positive aspect of respeto does enhance the aged's self-esteem. Thus, it stands to reason that this value is reinforced and practiced in the Center. The negative aspect is that respeto can be oppressive, lending itself to control. For example, in the Center, respeto controls who associates with whom (male to male, female to female, and female to male), who provides information and who receives it. The notion of respeto can essentially establish patterns of deference and subordination. Thus, the way in which respeto has been established in the Center is respect based on an age hierarchy, which applies to all outsiders to the Center. Most important, the aged have attempted to create a sense of mutual respect among women and men. This task has been one of their greatest challenges, given the reality of gender dynamics. This mutual respect between women and men has basically countered the controlling mechanism of respeto.

SUMMARY

Three major features characterized the Center:

- Celebration of life in the midst of the unpredictability and inevitability of the life course
- Women's groups and their subsequent impact on the Center's makeup
- Retention of various aspects of Chicano/Mexican culture

The Center allowed for the aged to accept the unpredictable and inevitable nature of the aging process. Celebrating life during monthly birthday parties was a triumph of survival. Health is a tangible factor, an issue that can be dealt with. Death, on the contrary, represents the intangible; life's daily struggles are confronted only by those who are fortunate to awake and successfully encounter a new day. The significance of birthday celebrations for Center participants is not the accumulation of chronological years, but continuing survival, a common historical struggle, and living into old age. Birthday celebrations provided the aged with the opportunity to congratulate and recognize one another for having survived as an immigrant and now as an older person.

The women's groups in the Center served as mechanisms for establishing a sense of self-worth and continuity, a means of supplementing monthly incomes, and a symbolic response to past male domination. These groups thus allow aged Chicanas to self-construct or self-define their old age. The structure and purpose of these women's groups is largely determined by age and gender dynamics. The need to establish a sense of self-worth is a direct response to an aging process that rarely grants the elderly a positive identity and defined status in society at large. In addition, these groups are a response to gender oppression, the devaluation of women in society. The activities and interactions that they employed were attempts to ensure a positive sense of identity as older Chicanas in the Center.

The very existence of the women's groups may be linked to the present social construction of old age. In other words, old age, as it is presently defined, may call for an expansion of skills and tasks associated with the private sphere. The durability of women's groups stemmed from continuous, active participation in a particular group, thus solidifying its existence. Competition, jealousy, and gossip were mechanisms of resistance. Such mechanisms were employed when a group's existence was threatened.

As patriarchy constrains women to the private sphere, their skills associated with this domain become viable during the later years, thus constituting distinct continuity. However, the same set of constraints that historically relegated women to low-paying jobs keeps them in poverty throughout old age. In conjunction with patriarchy, the principles of class and race/ethnicity influence the nature of old age for Chicanas. Thus, not only are Chicana elderly hindered by these factors, but they are rendered more vulnerable by the process of aging itself, which generates concerns of self-worth. Finally, these groups serve as a symbolic response to past male domination, thus allowing older Chicanas the opportunity to socially construct their old age.

With respect to cultural traditions, the Center was a place where Chicano/Mexican elderly reaffirmed cultural values that they felt were otherwise threatened. In particular, the cultural value of respeto was recognized and practiced in the Center. The Center provided an environment where the Chicano/Mexican elderly could age with a sense of pride and dignity. These people established the Center as a distinct world where they could openly welcome old age and deal with its contradictions accordingly.

It must be noted, however, that places such as the Center can reinforce and perpetuate the marginal social status of the aged. Centers, in general, do not integrate the aged into mainstream society, even if they provide an important mechanism for dealing with old age—they serve as "waiting zones" for the aged. Centers can be a person's last stop before death. However, Chicanos/Mexicans historically have been marginal to society. Chicano/Mexican aged are also now experiencing degrees of marginality in relationship to their families.

In sum, for Chicano elderly, Center life was established as a distinct world within the larger society. In some respects, Center life was thin and fragile. But its very existence emerged as a result of two conditions that characterize the members, continuities between past and present circumstances and social isolation. Classism, racism, and sexism have eroded their status throughout the life cycle, and the impact continues to be felt in later life. Several marked similarities exist between circumstances of members' adulthood and old age: immigrant experience, development of sound survival strategies, poverty, and political impotency—factors determined largely by class and race/ethnicity. Thus, it is not a great shock for the Chicano/Mexican aged to find themselves once more in difficult circumstances as they have endured many struggles.

After several months of observation and interaction with the seniors in the Center, I conducted the interviewing segment of my fieldwork. In the following, five composites of the women in the Center are presented. The experiences of Concepcíon Villegas, Antioñia Holquin, Berta Ramirez, Maria Gonzalez, and Mercedes Castillo will be discussed throughout the remainder of this book, representing the personas of older Chicanas encountered in the Center. These composites are intended to reflect and represent the views of all the women who were interviewed for this study.

PROFILES

Concepcíon Villegas

Concepcíon Villegas was born in 1923 in Sinaloa, Mexico. She attended school until the age of 10, then worked as a seamstress for 8 years. At the age of 18, in 1931, Concepcíon married and immigrated with her husband to Arizona, where all seven of her children were born. In our conversations about her children, she said how proud she was that her children were well-educated. Of her seven children, six either have a master's degree or are established professionals. Three of her seven children live in the city where she resides. The other four have relocated, primarily because of their jobs. Concepcíon's contact with her children is frequent, but primarily by telephone. She said they call every weekend and she spends the holidays with her children. Concepcíon said, *"Yo no tengo dificultades con ninguno de mis hijos"* (I don't have problems with any of my children).

Throughout her marriage, Concepcíon worked sporadically as a farm laborer, because her husband objected to her working outside the home. Consequently, Concepcíon received no work benefits for her past labor and was dependent on her husband's social security (survivor benefits), $455 a month. She has been widowed for 14 years. She lives alone in an older home, which was purchased shortly before her husband's death. She still makes a mortgage payment of $155 a month and said she has learned to live modestly. Concepcíon lives in an older Chicano/Mexican area, where poverty colors the neighborhood. Given its location, her home is threatened with gentrification. Also, homeowners in the neighborhood are being asked to relocate so that a hospital can be built, which ironically will not serve the Chicano/Mexican community.

Concepcíon was very energetic, her gestures were quick, sharp; her speech fast, direct, and high pitched. She took tremendous pride in her home and garden. She spent her weeknights with her neighbors, those who are Chicana/Mexicana. Concepcíon said that her next-door neighbor appears to be a very friendly woman. However, they were unable to communicate because Concepcíon speaks only Spanish and her neighbor only English. Attending Catholic church services on Sunday was a ritual. Concepcíon said that attending church is an obligation, and she feels uncomfortable if she does not attend regularly.

She was part of the Crochet Club at the Center and did some of the best work in the group. When she crocheted, she was fast, efficient, and extremely helpful to other group members. Physically, she was in good health. She was, however, a diabetic and had occasional arthritis in her arms. Like many of the other women, she attempted to camouflage her age, or as she said, to keep "from looking old." She kept herself fit, her hair dyed dark brown, and her cheeks colored with blush.

Antioñia Holquin

Antioñia was an attractive 78-year-old widow. She could not quite remember when she was born nor verify her birth with any legal document. After piecing together many incidents of her life, we concluded she was 78. Antioñia was slender with auburn-dyed hair. Her makeup was heavily applied on her warm, wrinkled face. Antioñia, also born in Mexico, "immigrated" to California in 1930 along with her husband. Antioñia only had a year of schooling in Mexico, as her labor power was needed to support the family. Shortly after 1933, her husband deserted her and their three children, two sons and a daughter. Later she met another man, with whom she lived for 16 years. Antioñia told me she did not marry this man because she was not sure if the husband who had deserted her earlier was still living. Years later, Antioñia learned of her husband's whereabouts and eventually of his death.

Antioñia has been living independently for nearly 20 years. She was very self-reliant and independent. She lived alone in a home she purchased with money earned as a domestic, a factory worker, and, during the last 20 years, as a cannery worker. Her home was old but well-kept. She lived in a Chicano barrio plagued by drugs and gang violence. Sirens late at night made her anxious because one of her sons was killed in a fight. Antioñia's son was apparently heavily intoxicated when a couple of men beat him to death in the parking lot of a neighborhood bar.

Antioñia was extremely active. She spent a tremendous amount of time with friends, frequenting local thrift shops, attending church, shopping at Woolworth's, eating at the local smorgasbord, and attending the Center. She attended Catholic church services every Sunday with her friends and afterward enjoyed a meal at a smorgasbord restaurant. Religion is very important to Antioñia, who believes her destiny is "in the hands of God."

Her relationships with her son and daughter were very good. They visited and called her frequently. During one of our interviews, her daughter made her daily call. Despite a minimal income of $425 a month and her children's willingness to help, Antioñia was insistent on remaining independent.

Antioñia, like Concepcíon, was active with the Crochet Club. She was always very helpful with the maintenance of the Center and assisted with Center activities whenever possible. Antioñia moved slowly but sturdily with her slender shoulders slightly hunched. Periodically, circulatory problems in her feet were painful, to the point where she cannot walk. Also, her diet was strict because, like many of the women in the Center, she was also diabetic.

Berta Ramirez

Berta Ramirez married at the age of 14 and after 53 years was still married. Born in 1921 in Guanejuato, Mexico, she came to the United States with her husband in 1935. Berta claimed never to have worked outside the home. She remembered several occasions when she cleaned windows for a ranch owner. Berta had 14 pregnancies, 11 ending in miscarriage. She attributed her miscarriages to poverty and subsequent illness. The Ramirezes' surviving three children live in the Midwest. The couple said they were not close to their children. They had infrequent contact, but, in general, their relationships with their children were cordial.

The Ramirezes lived in what is known as "the Projects." They feel very vulnerable because of the high crime rate in their neighborhood and their very limited understanding of English. Their apartment has been vandalized on several occasions. They described their day as active and religious. They recited the rosary every morning "to give thanks and to ask that God watch over us." Rarely did they miss attending the Center. Sra. Ramirez was an active member of the Altar Caretakers.

Sra. Ramirez had cataracts in both eyes and suffered from diabetes. Her health status was poor in comparison to Concepcíon and Antioñia. She was somewhat heavy and always very neatly and tastefully dressed, despite her poverty. At the Center, she slowly reapplied her facial powder and lipstick after the noon meal. Sra. Ramirez never failed to tend to the altar, nor to take the time to silently pray. She informed other Center members of local events sponsored by the Catholic church. Sra. Ramirez was well-informed not only of church activities but also about the priests and nuns affiliated with the church.

Maria Gonzalez

Maria Gonzalez, a 72-year-old widow, immigrated with her family in 1924 from Zacatecas, Mexico. She described how her family came in *secciónes,* or in various groups; first her father and uncles, her brothers, her aunts, then women with children. Their primary reason for immigrating to the United States was hunger. Maria began cooking at the age of 11 for her family, while they worked picking grapes. Maria completed 6 years of school in Mexico. However, Maria no longer attended school after she arrived in the United States because she was needed for household labor. At the age of 15, she began seasonal work in canneries and also picked cotton, peas, and strawberries until she married at the age of 20.

Maria lived with her 30-year-old daughter, the youngest of her five children. All but one of Maria's children lived in the vicinity, with her oldest child living in another state. Maria had frequent contact with all her children except one son, with whose wife she did not have a good relationship. It was primarily her daughters who visited and assisted her when needed.

Maria was diabetic and recovering quite well from a stroke she had suffered 2 years before my research. During our conversations, she would ask me if the paralysis on the left side of her face was noticeable. For the most part, Maria was very active. From time to time, I would see her on the bus or at a bus stop downtown. She said it was expensive to ride taxis and that bus service was unreliable. Like most of the Center members, she did not own a car nor did she know how to drive. Consequently, she was somewhat dependent on her children to help if she had a medical appointment or wanted to enjoy a day in the park. Despite these limitations, she said she did her best to enjoy herself. In particular, she enjoyed going out with her friends to eat and especially to the *cine Mexicano,* where Mexican films were shown.

Maria attended the Center regularly but did not get overly involved in any particular activity. She said her sight would not allow her to crochet as well as she once did, for example. She considered herself religious because she attends church regularly. Maria was part of the Center group referred to as the Socializers. She said she enjoys assisting in serving food and maintaining the Center.

Maria's home was comfortable, with pictures of her children and grandchildren decorating the walls. She lived in what is considered a high-crime area, which made her somewhat nervous about her own and her daughter's safety. Maria did not own the home she lived in; she had been a renter for about 10 years. She received $600 a month in survivor benefits. Maria said that the money she receives is sufficient because her daughter adds a small income, and her other children provide her with financial assistance when possible.

Mercedes Castillo

Mercedes was a 71-year-old widow and a mother of 10. It was always a pleasure to talk with Mercedes. She was very well-liked by all the seniors at the Center. She was kind and warm and treated her peers with respect. Mercedes was never one to involve herself in what she called "petty arguments." Mercedes was very diplomatic in her interactions with other Center members.

She was probably no more than 5 feet tall, with short, curly salt-and-pepper hair and a wide smile. Mercedes was in good physical condition, despite the fact that several months earlier, she had had a gallbladder operation. Walking was part of her daily exercise. Mercedes made every effort to walk to places within a reasonable distance, such as the grocery store, the Center, the Goodwill store, and restaurants.

Mercedes lived in a senior citizen apartment complex. There were over 100 elderly residents in this complex located near the Center. Mercedes enjoyed her living arrangement as it provided her the opportunity to interact with other residents. Mercedes's one-bedroom apartment was filled with beautiful green plants, pictures of her family, and four canaries.

Mercedes said that she was content with old age because of the support she received from her children. All but one of her 10 children lived in northern California. Mercedes said her children were not able to visit her on a regular basis because they were all very busy with work and their families. However, she had frequent telephone contact with them. But it was primarily her daughter, Graciela, who took her shopping, to church, to social events, and family get-togethers. Mercedes sadly spoke of one son who was an alcoholic. On several occasions, when he was drunk, he had been verbally abusive with Mercedes. Needless to say, Mercedes found his behavior extremely disrespectful, but she was also hurt by her son's occasional drunken outbursts. Consequently, Mercedes has very minimal contact with this particular son.

Mercedes was quite active in the Center. She helped coordinate the Socializers' work in setting up for the noon meal and serving lunches. Mercedes was also very talented with crocheting needles. However, she said it took too much time to crochet. She would much rather sit and talk with the other Center members and get involved in local cultural events. Mercedes was very active in community events such as Cinco de Mayo and the 16th of September and with events sponsored by the Catholic church. Mercedes considered herself to be religious as she attended church regularly on Sundays, and she was an active *Guadalupana*. In the course of my conversations with the women in the Center, I learned that poverty and economic vulnerability continued to be an issue for them. Poverty itself was not new to this population; they have experienced some degree of poverty since childhood. Thus, their poverty was not solely related to old age. The following chapter follows these five women outside the Center and focuses on how poverty affected or influenced their social construction or self-definition of old age.

NOTES

1. The terms *viejita* (elderly woman) and *viejito* (elderly man) are considered affectionate terms for older women and men.

2. See Macklin, J. 1990. El Niño Fidencio is considered a North Mexican folk saint who possesses great healing powers. For a more thorough discussion on La Virgin de Guadalupe, see Macklin and de Costilla (1979).

3

Being Old and Poor:
Structural Constraints in Chicana Old Age

Poverty among older Chicanas involves dependency on social programs for the aged poor, specifically Supplemental Security Income (SSI) and Medicaid. Nearly all the women in this study had been employed in the secondary labor market or service sector as farm workers, domestics, and cannery workers. Like other older Chicanas, they found that their past occupations provided little financial security in old age. Also, poverty for this population is characterized by an extreme vulnerability to poor health. Many women are primarily concerned with debilitating illnesses and becoming dependent and with whether their children will provide tangible financial assistance. Given their situation, older Chicanas develop a complex familial relationship with their children for both economic and cultural reasons. It is within the familial relationship that the older Chicana attempts to socially construct or define her old age, beyond the traditional role of *abuela* or grandmother.

It is important to first explore what contributes to the older Chicana's poverty so that we may better understand the limited options available to her in defining her old age. Second, in exploring the poverty situation, Chicanas' primary concern about health care becomes more apparent.

In general, elderly Latinos suffer a poverty rate of 27%, compared with a rate among the general elderly population of 10%.[1] Nearly 61% of older Latinas living alone have incomes below the poverty level (Traeuber, 1991). Older Chicanas represent 46% of all Chicano elderly living in poverty. Poverty and economic vulnerability among older Chicanos have not been critically assessed. Earlier discussions have often focused on the positive aspects of familism in describing and understanding the lives of older people (Coles, 1989; Markides et al., 1983; Mirande & Enriquez, 1979). Familism, as proposed in Chicano aging literature, comprises cultural values of family unity and expected mutual aid, respect for the aged, and a diminishing gender hierarchy. Regarding gender hierarchies, as people age, they gain in respect, and gender distinctions decrease. However, gender differences only become subsumed within the notion of respect.

Much of the literature tends to portray an extended family that supports and protects the aged from a "hostile" world. Maldonado (1985) argued that issues such as poverty and economic vulnerability were minimized by the "supportive qualities" of the Chicano family. Thus, poverty was largely overlooked because of the idealistic portrayal of the relationship between the Chicano family and the aged community.

Poverty for Chicana elderly is exacerbated in old age due to illness, retirement, marital status, or in some cases, unfortunate mishaps. For older Chicanas, poverty began in childhood, extended through marriages, and persists in widowhood and old age. In the more mainstream literature, economic conditions among the elderly are explained primarily as an outcome of age. Some authors argued that the middle and upper classes experienced a downward economic shift, thus placing many of these aged individuals in poverty for the first time in their lives. Age, however, is one of many factors that contributes to poverty among the elderly population in general in distinct and complex ways.

The following data illustrate how past marriages and work experiences have had cumulative effects on Chicanas in old age. Feminist theorists (Eisenstein, 1979; Hartmann, 1981; Kuhn & Wolpe, 1978; Milkman, 1992; Segura, 1986; Zavella, 1987) argued that the control of wage labor by capital is connected to men's control over women's labor power and sexuality in the home. Zavella (1987) said that job segregation is the primary mechanism that maintains the domination of men over women, for example, by enforcing lower wages for women. Second, "women's labor-market activities are restricted through the bearing and rearing of children and men's efforts to control home life" (Zavella, 1987, p. 3).

Like most women, many older Chicanas have interrelated experiences in the home and the labor market. For example, 28 of the 30 women interviewed for this study said they had been employed in the labor market prior to their marriages. Only two women claimed they had no work experience outside the home. Once married, 24 of the 28 women who had been previously employed no longer worked. A few worked temporarily during extreme economic hardships. Only two women continued to work after they were married.

Slightly more than half of the women were forced into the labor market as a result of desertion or marital separation. Only two women in the sample were divorced. One was divorced in her early 30s and the other in her 50s. More specifically, 16 of the 30 women became primary wage earners due to marital dissolution. Their occupational histories date back to the late 1930s and early 1940s spanning a 30- to 50-year period.

Others were largely confined to the home after marriage. For 12 of the 30 women in this study, poverty in old age could largely be traced to inequalities experienced in the home. These women have been widowed within the last 10 years and are referred to as "late widows" because they became widowed late in their marriages and also in old age.

LATE WIDOWS: FROM INDEPENDENT WORKER TO DEPENDENT SPOUSE

Late widows described their past marriages as traditional, with their primary responsibilities being child care and household maintenance. Rarely did they work outside the home. A strong sense of spousal dependency developed and continued throughout their marriages until widowhood. Nearly all late widows worked in factories, as farm workers, or as domestics before being married. Once married, their husbands demanded they quit work, take care of the children, and keep the house.

Of the five composites, Concepción willingly shared her life experiences as a housewife, as she sat in a newly upholstered chair. Her home was very clean, cool, and dark. She lived in what is considered a low-income area. She complained, telling me with fear in her voice that her social security checks had been stolen from her mailbox. Her home, built in the late 1930s or early 1940s, appears small from the outside. A detached one-car garage sits in the back of the house. The driveway is not cement but packed dirt. But the environment is beautified by large trees that hang over the house and a garden of bold green plants and assorted flowers growing along the cyclone fence. Evidently she gives great care to her yard and garden.

Concepción's home was cozy but orderly. Every piece of furniture and knickknack was organized in such a way that nothing seemed out of place. The curtains were drawn to keep the hot sun from warming the living room. Pictures of her children and grandchildren adorned the walls. The living room was large, with arched doorways leading to the bedroom and the dining room. A vintage radio is kept in the small dining room, along with a more modern combination stereo/television set. It reminded me of the first television set my parents bought when I was 8 years old. Throughout the house, tables were covered with white and turquoise doilies that had been stiffened with corn syrup, sugar, and water. House plants filled the dining room, nearly covering the full-length windows. The table, with a white linen cloth and plastic covering, held a large white ceramic bowl and pitcher. I sat comfortably in the dining room with Concepcíon, drinking a Cragmont soda and eating *pan dulce* (Mexican sweet bread), listening to her reconstruct her past.

Her work experiences are characteristic of late widows who began working as young girls. Concepcíon moved from being an independent working girl to being a mother and dependent spouse. She currently receives $465 a month in survivor's benefits (spouse's social security) and $84 from SSI, a federal cash assistance program for the aged poor. Concepcíon said,

> I went to school until the age of 10. Then I had to go to work because I had my mother and my brother, and you know how hard life is in Mexico. So I worked for 8 years in a factory making quilts. I was used to working and being independent, earning my own money, until I got married. My husband didn't like me working. He said it wasn't necessary for me to work . . . just in the house, taking care of the children, washing, ironing, cooking.

Maria described a similar experience:

> I worked before I got married. When I was 11 or 12, I cooked for the family, and they worked picking grapes. Then I worked in Los Angeles when I was 17 or 18 in a canning company. I worked until I was 20—that's when I got married. I was picking cotton, peas, and working in the straw-berries. Two months after I got married, I became pregnant . . . My husband didn't want me to work. When the baby came, he told me, "If you want to work, who's going to take care of the baby?" I said, "maybe I'll look for a baby-sitter." He said, "You think a baby-sitter is better than a mother? I work . . . you don't have to work . . . the mother is better for the child . . . you'd be better than anybody else." So he didn't let me work . . . I raised my child and took care of the house and everything . . . I did a lot.

Late widows who were unemployed during their marriages expressed some resentment toward their husband's dominance. They rationalized their past situations by referring to traditional socialization of women. The ideology of women's "proper place" is that women are moral guardians of the home and therefore should not enter the labor force. Women's family responsibilities should consist of housework, child care, consumption, and emotional nurturance. Concepción said, "Men didn't believe in women working. We were taught that the woman was for the house. Now a lot of women work and have children. . . . yeah, times have changed a lot, but not the way we think."

Concepción's anecdote about work captured the frustrations and subsequent strategies employed in conventional marital arrangements.

> I wanted to work but he [husband] didn't let me. When we were in Fresno, there was a lot of work picking tomatoes. The other women would come from work and tell me, "I made $25, I made $30, I made $15" and I would say, "Oh no, I don't want to hear it!" . . . the next day, I put on a pair of pants, a bandana, gloves, and everything, and my husband said, "Where are you going?" . . . "I'm going to pick tomatoes," . . . "No, take off those pants."

Concepción laughed and cried as she reenacted the discussion she had with her husband about work. Her frustration at the repression she experienced surfaced in the remainder of her anecdote.

> I wanted to earn some money, just to have extra money. There was a big wash room [in the labor camp] and this is where all the women would talk about how much money they made. So one day, when they [her husband and children] had all gone to work or school, I had a little baby girl, she was about 6 months, she was small. I dressed her with little booties, a hat, and everything and I took her with me. On the other side of the field, on the other side of where we lived, we lived in the camps, you know, like concentration camps, we lived over there in the barracks. Where we lived there were big fences, they were like doors to the field.
> I took a bunch of bottles and diapers, and I took her with me in a hurry to the field. I went and made about $25 picking tomatoes, but then it started to rain. The women said to me, "Come on, Concha, you're going to get sick." "No," I told them, "I just want to keep my baby covered [from the rain]. Can you do me a favor so I can finish working?" They put the baby in a car in her little basket, and I put a sweater on, and I finished work.

When I came home there was no food for dinner [laughing, she got up from her chair and reenacted the entire scene as though it had just happened yesterday] . . . what saved me is that I cooked a lot of meat the night before. But I didn't know if there would be enough with seven kids, then my husband. Can you imagine! So I had some meat already cooked and there I was. I tenderized it real fast (she pretended she was at the stove tenderizing the meat). I put it on the stove cooking with onion and opened three cans of string beans, mixed it with a can of tomatoes. I put the dinner on the table with coffee, but I didn't have any milk. So there I go running to borrow some milk from a neighbor. I told her, "I ran out of milk, can I borrow some and I'll pay you back." And here I come from the back with the milk.

Then my husband said, "You're up to something, what did you do?" [She laughed so hard, she could barely continue with her story.] . . . I was so scared, nervous, running through the house like I was crazy . . . "I didn't do anything daddy, I didn't do anything." "Yes, you did. Tell me what you did." [She broke into uncontrollable laughter.] . . . After dinner the kids studied and the little baby she couldn't talk so I was OK.

And what did she do with the $25?

They didn't pay me. [We broke into hysterics, given all she went through—for nothing. She returned to her dinner story.] . . . There I was all night with my heart jumping, and my husband said again, "You did something. Tell me the truth, did the baby fall?" "No," I said. "What did you do, did you buy something?" "No, I'm going to tell you the truth, but don't get mad." "No, I won't get mad." "I went to pick tomatoes." He got mad. He said I wasn't starving, I had clothes, and what more did I want. I told him I just wanted to earn the money. But you know what happened when they took the tomatoes to the cannery? They rejected [them] because it rained too hard, that's why the boss didn't pay me. . . . That's what he told me. After all that . . . [Again we broke into hysterics.]

Concepcíon's narrative speaks to the dissatisfaction she felt in not being able to work. Her dissatisfaction had to do not only with work but also with the fact that someone else determined her role in the marriage. Concepcíon said she wanted to contribute to the family economically, but her husband objected on the grounds that it was the male's responsibility to economically provide for the family.

In addition, her narrative also illustrates how women in marital conflicts employ a number of strategies, such as manipulation and dishonesty, and fear the risks or repercussions of their acts (Pesquera, 1993, pp. 191-195). Even though many women rationalize their situations with traditional ideologies of work, they do not necessarily agree that women should be excluded from the labor force. However, most feel the home is primarily a woman's responsibility. These comments reflect traditional socialization about women's relationship to the home. This apparent contradiction of women in the home and the labor market mirrors societal messages about women as caregivers/homemakers and workers. Women, for the most part, are accepted as workers, but only women are primarily considered as caregivers and/or homemakers.

UNPARTNERED WIDOWS: FROM DEPENDENT SPOUSE TO PRIMARY WAGE EARNER

The remaining 16 of the 30 women interviewed are referred to as "unpartnered widows."[2] These women were either deserted by their husbands or were separated or divorced before they were actually widowed; they claimed widowhood upon knowledge of their former husband's death. Unpartnered widows called themselves widows rather than separated or divorced women in order to avoid the stigma attached to dissolved marriages. Because of their traditional views on marriage, separation and divorce were not favorably regarded among this community of elderly. Furthermore, dissolved marriages were analogous to failure as a wife.

The economic predicament of unpartnered widows in old age is largely related to their previous occupations. Because of early marital dissolution, these women were forced into the secondary labor market as primary wage earners. They were young mothers and single heads of households with children in poverty.

During a visit at her home, Antoñia spoke proudly of her work history. She worked in various canneries for the last 15 years of her work life—until the age of 73—in order to pay off her mortgage. At the time of the interview, she was 82. Antoñio sat comfortably in an older home in a high-crime neighborhood. Like Concepcíon's, Antoñia's home was clean and tidy. A large picture of the Virgin Mary in an oval woodlike frame hung above the doorway to the bedroom. Crucifixes, wrapped with rosaries, along with pictures of her children and grandchildren decorated her home. Her talent with crocheting needles was displayed with afghans covering her living room furniture. The couch and matching loveseat were soft and comfortable. We began our conversation in the living room and eventually moved to the small kitchen, seating ourselves at the small gray and white speckled table with two matching chairs. As we began the interview, I was offered something to eat. This was the common overture to most interviews. I began drinking a soda, eating a pastry, and reluctantly nibbling at some vanilla ice cream. Eventually, I saw that I would have to eat beans, tortillas, and *fideo,* Mexican-prepared vermicelli, as Antoñia realized that a few hours had passed, and it was almost time for dinner.

Antoñia and her three young children had been deserted by her husband shortly before the Depression. She and her children were living with her mother and her mother's husband when the Depression hit. Antoñia was forced to seek employment in a nearby town. She described her experience in these terms:

> There was a great Depression when I left . . . but what was I going to do with my kids and no help, my family couldn't help me, my mother, my sister . . . so I went to work for the rich . . . They paid me $.25 an hour. I used to clean their homes, wash the windows. I had just had my daughter. . . . I remember going to work with my breasts aching. . . . It was so hard during that time. We really suffered.

It was especially difficult for Antoñia to survive because of her limited job skills. This made it very hard to find a job that would provide substantial support for her and her children. After the Depression, Antoñia worked in a laundry.

> In the early [19]40s, I went to work in a laundry owned by Chinese. They paid me about $18.00 a week. I was only there for a couple of months. I used to iron and fold sheets. Then I took care of women who were sick . . . they didn't pay me very much, only $1.25 a day, so I went to work for SP (Southern Pacific) for 4 years, '41-'44. That was really hard work, pounding nails, carrying pieces of plastic and metal. I used to come home so sore, aching all over, that was a man's job! After that, in '45, I went to work in the cannery. I worked in different canneries for 26 years, but only temporarily. I didn't work full-time. That's why I don't get much from social security, I used to make $.65 an hour, then later after a lot of years, $3 an hour. Then I worked 8 years in a frozen food plant. At the plant, I used to work the worst hours. Sometimes they would call us at 1 in the morning to start work at 3 . . . . after a while I said to myself, "I can't do this anymore." I was 73 when I left work because I wanted to pay off my house, and I

could retire because of my age. All that hard work made me very tired. I worked so hard and I barely get $400 a month.

Mercedes Castillo went in and out of the labor force. While married, she did not work because her husband insisted that child care be her primary responsibility.

> I didn't work when I was married to my husband because he said I had to take care of the children. But once I was alone, I worked in a lot of different jobs. It was really hard, because now I had to work to support my family. It wasn't like it is now, at least there's welfare. But before, they didn't give you anything, so I had to work to survive. I had never worked before, because my husband didn't let me, so I struggled to survive. People helped me to find jobs and taught me how to work. The women that used to work picking cucumbers and tomatoes, they used to show me how to do the work. Then I figured out a way to get government assistance for my children. The Red Cross helped me out a lot, too. I used to get beans and sugar. Sometimes I would get boxes of food for my kids. I worked mainly in the fields picking cotton, grapes, tomatoes, lettuce, peas. I worked on the tomato machines and in the canneries. I don't get social security because I didn't work long enough in the cannery. I think you have to work 9 or 10 years in one cannery to get checks. I get SSI.

Mercedes received $560 a month from SSI. She lived in an eight-story senior citizen apartment complex near the Center. From the inside, the building seemed secure, but it was located in a poverty-stricken neighborhood. Her apartment was small, but cozy. The living room was filled with plants, pictures of her family, and three small bird cages with yellow canaries. After the interview, we shared a cup of coffee and fed the birds. Mercedes then took me around the building, introducing me to other residents, telling them of my work, and acknowledging me as her friend.

Repercussions of gender inequities experienced in both the home and the labor market are well actualized in old age. Gender imbalances in the home result in women as dependent caregivers and housekeepers, making transitions to widowhood difficult. Late widows experience an abrupt transition from a state of dependency to an expected state of independence. Here is how Concepcíon recalled the transition.

> Well, I went through a great change in that I never thought I would be able to buy the food, pay the bills, to do nothing. He made himself responsible

for everything. So I had to learn how to pay the bills. So when he passed away, it was really hard for me. I thought the ceiling fell on my head.

For the first time, many late widows are solely responsible for the entire upkeep of their homes and a household income. Maintaining their homes is a major task, as most of these homes are some 40 to 50 years old. Consequently, they have high maintenance costs, not to mention utility expenses and property taxes. Navarro and Berman (1984) said, "this leaves many of the aged on small fixed incomes with insufficient money left for the meeting of other basic needs" (p. 38).

The responsibility in sustaining an adequate household income is of greatest concern. Overall, 4 of the 12 late widows in this study were entitled to either their spouse's pension or social security benefits. More specifically, one woman received her husband's pension benefits, and 3 received social security benefits. The remaining 7 women were dependent on SSI.

Many late widows are not entitled to survivor benefits because of the types of jobs their husband's held. Based on their class and race/ethnicity, these men were segregated to occupations in the secondary labor market. Two thirds (66%) of elderly Latinos have worked in the service, unskilled, and farm sectors, compared with 40% of all elderly. Elderly Chicanos are more likely than members of other Latino groups to have worked in the farm sector (17%) or the service sector (20%). These jobs are frequently without pension plans or survivor benefits. This substantially eliminates the late widow's opportunity to receive spousal benefits in the form of economic support.

Thus, late widows suffer a double burden. First, with the onset of widowhood, they lose a steady source of income. Second, because of their husband's former occupation, they are less likely to receive either pension or social security benefits. Consequently, for a great majority of late widows, their monthly incomes are supplemented or fully compensated by SSI. Their dependency is now shifted onto the state, as their economic welfare hinges upon federal cash assistance programs.

Unlike late widows, unpartnered widows did not experience an actual transition into widowhood. Widowhood did not bring about new responsibilities of maintaining a home nor a household income. Widowhood, if anything, is more symbolic for this group. By this I mean widowhood is a status that provides a sense of identity and position among their cohort.

However, poverty is a prevalent feature of their old age. Of the 16 women who had work histories in the paid labor force, only 4 received social security benefits. The monthly payments awarded to these women ranged from $57 to $254. One woman was receiving $119 a month, after nearly 20 years of work as a seamstress. Two received $57 and $114 a month for cannery work, and one received $185 a month for civil service work.

After nearly 30 to 50 years of hard labor, these women were granted meager social security benefits. The other 12 women, also with work histories, were dependent on SSI. In other words, they received no social security benefits for their past work.

Employment in the secondary labor market as domestics, farm workers, or factory and cannery workers has tremendous economic consequences for Chicanas in old age. Under current social security provisions, jobs previously held by some unpartnered widows were not formally recognized as contributory work production. The Social Security Act of 1935 and the defeat of the Wagner-Murray-Dingell bills throughout the 1940s reinforced and codified into federal law two levels of distinction in social welfare programs. The Social Security Act comprised a group of programs that would provide federal support only for the "deserving poor," those who were poor through some misfortune that was beyond their control: people who were too old to work, the blind, and those with disabilities that prevent them from working, dependent widows and children, and those who truly could not find work. All others who might be indigent, including the *working poor* and people who did not work for reasons other than those included in the act, were considered "undeserving" of federal relief and were left to the resources and charity of the states, local governments, and private agencies.

Consequently, unpartnered widows were regarded as the "underserving poor." Thus, rather than being compensated for their past contributions with pensions, retirement benefits, or social security, punitive actions in the form of federal cash assistance programs (SSI) are overwhelming distributed to this population.

Being old and widowed does not necessarily bring about poverty for aged Chicanas. The data indicate that previous life circumstances among late and unpartnered widows intensify economic conditions in old age. The predicament of late widows in old age is largely influenced by previous marital relationships characterized by a strict division of labor that shaped their lives. Their primary responsibilities consisted of child care and household maintenance, and they generally did not work outside the home. This rigid division of labor by gender, which generates female dependency, is a major obstacle in dealing with transitions to widowhood.

Widowhood brings on new responsibilities, requiring these women to take an active part in situations that are not part of their prior experience. Second, division of labor by gender greatly contributes to their poverty in old age. Widowhood means sole responsibility for their economic welfare. The situation is intensified because these women have no previous work experience considered of value. Their efforts as young children and teenagers in unskilled, service sectors and later in the home is not considered productive work. These jobs do not allow for them to pay into any type of social security system or insurance program. Those Chicanas who are widowed in old age find themselves largely dependent on SSI, rarely awarded spousal benefits, and living in or near the brink of poverty.

Unpartnered widows who separate or divorce early in their marriages do not experience a transition to widowhood. What they do experience is forced entry into the labor market. Even though these women were employed, the types of occupations they held do not guarantee any security for old age. In other words, social security does not benefit or reward individuals for cannery work, farm work, factory work, or domesticity, work performed in the unskilled, service sector.

Distinctions made by class, race/ethnicity, and gender in the labor market have repercussions for Chicanas well into old age. This notion is supported by a report from the Select Committee on Aging, House of Representatives (1988), which reports that minority elderly are far more likely to be poor or near poor than white elderly. The income of women of all races is lower than that of men of all races, but both white men and white women have higher incomes than minority elderly of their own gender.

The sources of income for minorities are also different from those of other elderly. Minority elderly are far less likely to receive pensions or other retirement income. They are, therefore, much more likely to rely on social security as their primary source of income. However, minority men are more likely to be dependent on social security. The poverty situation for elderly Chicanas with work histories is further distinguished by their substantial dependence on SSI rather than social security. The injustice to Chicana elderly who have been employed in jobs segregated by class, race/ethnicity, and gender is reflected in their overwhelming dependence on SSI.

Despite the fact that Chicanas have worked in paid and/or unpaid labor sectors, they are not guaranteed financial security in old age. With the exception of two women, all the elderly Chicanas in this study worked before marriage, primarily as domestics and farm workers. The women in this study are distinguished only by the varying circumstances that contribute to their poverty. Regardless of their economic contributions— whether they are considered "work" or not, "productive" or not—ultimately these women share the common life experience of poverty in old age. Redclift and Mingione (1985) addressed how such terms as *family labor* or *part-time work* or *domestic* work can all be used as synonyms for the unpaid work of women and children, serving to mask rather than illuminate crucial aspects of the relations of production. Thus, the very terms that describe diverse modes of production are defined within a class and patriarchal context serving to determine who is rewarded and who is not in old age.

Older Chicanas have experienced the repercussions of an economic system that has only been concerned with their labor output and has had very little regard for their immediate and future quality of life. Various scholars have provided both documentation and analyses of the Chicana's subjugation to discriminatory practices in the labor force, dating back to the annexation of northern Mexico in 1848. Barrera (1979) said the use of wage differentials based on race and sex was common throughout the Southwest and continued into the 20th century. Zavella (1987) showed how Chicana workers, especially in border towns, were victimized by receiving lower wages than Anglo women received for the same work. Garcia (1989) reported that Chicana urban workers experienced poor working conditions and miserable wages as domestics and laundresses and as workers in food-processing industries (Ruiz, 1982) and in Los Angeles factories (Taylor, 1981).

The point to be made regarding Chicana labor experiences is that a substantial number of Chicanas (as well as Chicanos) have remained at the bottom of the working class for more than a century. According to data from the National Chicano Survey, about 78% of Chicano workers had working-class occupations. Thus, an economic system concerned only with profit rather than the plight of humanity has left this population, like many others in U.S. society, in a most difficult situation. In addition, patriarchy has contributed to the older Chicana's present poverty.

As older Chicanas experience downward shifts in actual monthly income, for the most part, they experience a lateral rather than hierarchical change in their quality of living. Financial priorities shift from feeding, clothing, and educating children to personal health and rent. In particular, older Chicanas feel susceptible to further impoverishment with respect to the high probability of chronic illnesses. Verbrugge (1985) reported that women were more likely to experience higher morbidity from acute conditions and nonfatal chronic disease such as varicose veins, gallbladder conditions, thyroid conditions, anemias, migraines, and chronic urinary disease. Also more common for women were hypertensive disease, hemorrhoids, chronic bronchitis, and arthritis. In a recent study by Cuellar (1990), he reported that diabetes and arthritis were the most common illnesses among older Chicana populations.

With age, health-related problems increase, while money to sufficiently tend to health needs becomes minimal. Furthermore, Chicana aged are more concerned with whether family members will be able to assist them during their time of need. For example, Maria said,

> When I'm sick, it bothers me to be old, but otherwise I pay my bills. . . . the only thing that makes me think, is if I'm an invalid or something, where is the money going to come from and will there be someone to take care of me?

Declining health is of great concern to all elderly people. Given the substantial economic disadvantages and considerable health problems experienced by many elderly Chicanos/Latinos, it is not surprising that many have said they worry about not having enough money. They worry about their medical bills and becoming dependent on their families. They are, however, dependent on government safety nets such as Medicaid and SSI, although many who are eligible may not be receiving these benefits. They clearly articulate the difficulty and challenge of living on fixed, but minimal, incomes. Mercedes spoke to this issue:

> I don't spend money on anything else, only on what's necessary. I spend my money on food and on my bills, the telephone, electricity, and gas. The thing we [aged Chicanos] worry about is our health. Who's going to pay for the bills and will we have someone to take care of us? We have to buy what is necessary, we can't have expensive tastes. When we get our checks, the important thing is to pay our bills, then buy food.

For most elderly in the United States today, health costs are a major concern. With current budget cuts and the elimination of social programs directed toward the elderly, accessibility to proper health care is becoming increasingly difficult. The for-profit health care monopolies encourage and exacerbate discriminatory practices in a multitude of ways. For example, the dangerous practice of "dumping" low-income patients into public hospitals is an attack on minorities, moving hospitals out of the area or building new health care facilities that do not serve the community. To add another obstacle, sexism further excludes women, and especially women of color, from receiving quality health care. The corporate pursuit of profits instead of health care, politically, economically, and ideologically, has had a devastating effect on the health care of the nation, particularly the health of minority, low-income working people, children, the aged, and the unemployed.

Older Chicanos have the highest rate of poverty among the Hispanic subgroups, yet they are the least likely to be covered by Medicaid or to receive SSI.[3] In general, elderly Chicanos and Latinos face serious health and long-term care problems. They are more likely than the overall elderly population to be in fair or poor health and to be functionally impaired (54% of elderly Chicanos/Latinos report fair or poor health compared with 35% of all elderly). Poverty and poor health are closely associated: Fifty-eight percent of poor elderly Chicanos/Latinos are in fair or poor health, compared with 46% of those who are not poor.[4]

Compounding the problem of poor health is the lack of adequate financial protection against the high cost of medical care. Medicaid rules exclude many Chicanos/Latinos. Unlike Medicare, Medicaid is means-tested: Only people making less than a certain amount, which varies from state to state, qualify. Those tests tend to be one of two categorical programs, Aid to Families with Dependent Children (AFDC) or SSI. Eligibility is linked directly to the poverty level, $12,100 for a family of four. SSI requirements also vary by state. In California, for example, SSI benefits range from $500 to $550.

Thus older Latinos are more likely to rely on their families for assistance with acute and long-term health care. The problem, however, is whether or not families are able or willing to provide such support. Given older Chicanas' vulnerable health and their limited resources, options available to this population in socially constructing their old age are minimal. Because of the interdependent relationship between the aged and their children, the family becomes the institution in which the older Chicana attempts to define her old age. Several complex factors are involved with health-related familial support among older Chicanas and their families. In the following chapter, the older Chicana's relationship to her family and her subsequent redefinition of herself as an older Chicana is explored.

NOTES

1. About 33% of Latino elderly, compared with 18% of older whites, hover just above the "near poverty" threshold at incomes below 125% of the poverty line. The median personal income of Latinos age 65 and over is about 65% of the income enjoyed by white males their age; for Latinas age 65 and over, the median income is 68% of what white females their age have to spend (U.S. Senate Special Committee on Aging, 1992).

2. Julia Curry Rodriguez (1988), in her study of undocumented female Mexican workers, coined this term in categorizing "marital" statuses among this population.

3. Only 83% receive Medicare benefits compared with 96% of the elderly generally (Kasper, 1988).

4. The poverty of older Latinos is undoubtedly a major factor in their generally poor health, with 85% of older Latinos reporting at least one chronic condition and 45% reporting some limitation on activities of daily living. Physiological aging tends to precede chronological aging, with those in their late forties experiencing health disabilities typical of 65-year-old whites. Arthritis, high blood pressure, circulatory disorders, diabetes, cataracts, glaucoma, and heart disease are the most common health problems (Cuellar, 1990).

4

Familial Relationships
and Chicana Old Age

The extent to which the Chicano family acts as a support for Chicano/
Mexican aged is a major theme in Chicano aging literature (Facio &
Wallace, 1988). Generally, works focus on the relationship between familial support and the aged's psychological well-being: life satisfaction,
morale, self-esteem, and so on. In this study, families included the participants' children and grandchildren. In many cases, *compadres* or co-
parents (relationships established through the religious ceremony of
baptism) were also considered part of familial networks. The major con-
clusions drawn are that most aged parents live with their children and
subsequently only have contact with their immediate families. In fact,
Latino elderly are less likely to live alone *or* with a spouse than are other
elderly people.[1] Nearly one third of elderly Latinos live with children,
siblings, other relatives, or unrelated people, compared with only 16% of
all elderly (Westat, 1989).

These general statistics, however, do not account for variation among
Latino elderly populations nor gender differences in living arrangements.[2] With respect to women, the American Association of Retired
Persons (1991) estimated that more than 80% of the nearly 9 million
Americans age 65 and older living alone are women. In addition, the
circumstances under which elderly people live with children were not
specified. For example, elderly people may live with children because of
low incomes and/or because their health and functional status is so poor
that they are unable to cope without assistance.

Furthermore, the literature implies that the elderly are dependent on
their children and that children unconditionally provide instrumental,

77

financial, emotional, and social support for aged parents. The reality of familial relationships is not considered. Also, the feelings and reactions of the elderly vis-à-vis their families and vice versa are rarely examined. In this study, further review of the data reveals a complex interdependent relationship between older Chicanas and their children.

The interdependent relationship between older Chicanas and their families is largely shaped by economic status, familism, and the social construction of gender. As proposed in the previous chapter, older Chicanas are likely to turn to their families for assistance with health care-related matters. Because of their poverty, elderly Chicanas are more vulnerable to poor health and to health-related dependency on their children. A second factor involved in this relationship is that of familism. According to Baca Zinn and Eitzen (1990), close kinship ties among Chicanos are often labeled familism and are presumed to be a defining family characteristic. According to the authors,

> The structure and function of Chicano families is characterized by 1) a strong and persistent familistic orientation; 2) a widespread existence of highly integrated extended kinship systems even for Chicanos who are three or more generations removed from Mexico; and 3) the consistent preference for relying on the extended family for support as the primary means for coping with emotional stress. (p. 124)

David Maldonado (1981) argued that familism includes respect for the aged, manifested in forms of obligatory assistance to aged family members, in particular one's parents. Family unity is realized by the practice of mutual aid within the family. According to Maldonado, the family is viewed as a life-long system of emotional support and, at times, material assistance. This is especially true with respect to the aged; children are expected to provide for their parents when they reach old age.

Many women said they expected their children to provide both financial assistance and emotional support, especially during times of illness. For example, Maria said,

> It's an obligation for children to respect their parents, because when they're younger, we struggle with them, and when we're older, they have to struggle with us. That's the way it should be. When we get sick, I think our children should care for us, not put us away so they don't have to bother with us.

Not providing this expected and obligatory assistance is considered an act of disrespect. Thus the dependent nature of the older Chicana's relationship with her children stems from her lack of sufficient economic resources and from familism, namely values of respect for the aged displayed through instrumental support. Interestingly, health-related dependency of elderly Chicanas' on their families in turn solidifies familial relationships and the notion of respect for the aged. The very manifestation of this value is reinforced and solidified through the obligatory assistance provided by the family.

No doubt, the relationship between older Chicanas and their families is dependent upon their children's economic situation and whether or not a positive relationship between family members exists. As a case in point, in this study, one woman noted that she did not have a positive relationship with her family because only one of her five children communicated with and visited her regularly. Another woman also indicated that she and her husband had minimal contact with their children because of strained relationships. For the most part, however, the women said they had close relationships with their children.

Older Chicanas are now experiencing an element of independence from their family, as well. Like many families in today's society, Chicano families are experiencing various forms of structural change as they attempt to adjust to an advanced technological society (Williams, 1990, p. 6). As society becomes more technologically sophisticated, demands for highly skilled workers are increasing. This, however, excludes a large portion of Chicanos, who are not educationally prepared and are thus largely relegated to occupations in blue-collar and service sectors. Bonacich (1980) said that only 27% of white employees fell into these categories, compared with 47% of African Americans and 43% of Latinos (pp. 101-102).

A large number of Chicano households have dual wage earners primarily but not solely out of economic necessity. Bonacich (1980) reported that the median weekly earnings of white families in 1986 was $566, compared to $412 for Latino families and $391 for African American families (p. 101). Many workers face occupational setbacks in the form of inadequate health insurance, layoffs, and unemployment. Unemployment rates in 1987 were reported at 10.5% for Latinos and 10.8% for Latinas (U.S. Department of Labor, 1987). Skyrocketing housing costs and educational expenses are also pinching the pockets of Chicano families.

With respect to single Chicanas, the situation appears to be worsening, as blue-collar jobs disappear and the number of single-mother families rises. Amott and Matthaei (1991) said that "between 1978 and 1987, the poverty rate in the Chicana/o community rose from 21% to 28%" (p. 91). Teenage pregnancy was also affecting the structure of the Chicano family. Many women in their late 30s and early 40s are now grandparents themselves. These women—what is referred to as the "sandwich" generation—may have to care not only for aged parents, but also for their children and many times their grandchildren. Women in general face multiple, cross-generational demands along with employment responsibilities. More women are employed than in the past. For example, 62% of women between the ages of 45 and 54, and 42% of women between the ages of 55 and 64, are in the workforce. Employed daughters provide nearly as much care for parents as nonemployed daughters (Brody & Schoonover, 1986).

These factors undoubtedly affect the type of assistance children are able to provide their aged parents. Hence, there is little opportunity for aged parents to become fully dependent on their children (whether they would like to or not), given these socioeconomic conditions. Nonetheless, even within situations that can be quite confining, familism also influences how children will respond to the needs of their aged parents.

In general, Chicanos feel obligated to care for their aged parents. The cultural value of respect for the aged is a value that is embedded in their upbringing. Many Chicanos may feel distressed in caring for their parents because their own economic situation may seem tenuous. Others simply do not want to be bothered. Many, of course, care for their aged parents out of affection, responsibility, and/or moral obligation. Again, as previously mentioned, lack of support and assistance to aged parents is regarded as an act of disrespect among the older Chicano community.

Two other factors that also shape the independent nature of the older Chicanas' relationship to her children is an entitlement to Supplemental Security Income (SSI). In old age, Chicanas are reinstated with steady incomes in the form of spousal benefits, social security, and/or SSI. Regardless of the minimal amounts received, this allows for some financial independence. For example, many aged Chicanas do not need to live with their children, and many in this study chose not to for reasons that will be discussed later in the chapter. Finally, life expectancy has increased among Chicana aged. Subsequently, this population is living longer in comparison with prior generations of older Chicanas. This has provided an opportunity for older Chicanas to create and define old age beyond and outside tradition.

Socioeconomic factors and familism interact to create both the dependent and independent nature of the older Chicana's relationship to her children. The scenario is incomplete without referring to this familial relationship from the position of the older Chicana's children.

The children of older Chicanas are dependent on their parents first, for child care and second, as a source of cultural reinforcement. With the high costs of day care centers, many working Chicana mothers turn to their aged mothers for child care assistance. Second, because of the lack of ethnic and cultural reinforcement in child care centers, Chicano families feel assured that their child(ren) will be exposed to Chicano culture mainly in the form of food, language, music, and cultural values such as respect for parents and grandparents.

It is also worth noting social and financial forms of assistance or displays of familism. For example, social forms of assistance and support include visiting, shopping, attending church, and so on. With respect to monetary assistance, some older Chicanas receive financial help with rent and monthly bills. Gifts or items of necessity such as small furnishings and clothes are also given to aged parents. Others have been asked to live with their children.

A primary characteristic of the older Chicana's familial relationship with her children is rooted in assistance and support with health-related situations. The complexity of this relationship is best understood in terms of her socioeconomic status and familism. Children's response to the needs of aged parents is shaped by their own economic situation as well as expectations associated with familism. Furthermore, children of older Chicanas look to parents as means of cultural continuity and preservation.

The five profiles of women presented in Chapter 2 illustrate the interdependent relationship between older Chicanas and their children. Ultimately, I propose that familial relationships among older Chicanas and their children are currently experiencing ideological as well as structural transitions.

When questioned about familial relationships, the women responded that familial networks should rest on mutual assistance. More specifically, all family members should assist one another in times of need, financially, socially, and/or emotionally. Generally, this view is also held by the women's children. Assistance is viewed as a familial obligation, a family duty. Familial networks are considered the primary means of assistance during illness. For example, when stricken with an illness, these women first call their immediate families. For example, Concepcíon said,

> I have these women [at the Center], but I first call my daughter. So, I really don't need them in that way, because the one person I call right away is my daughter. I remember one time I fell coming out of Church. I sprained my ankle. My daughter came every day to prepare my meals, just to see what I needed, and there she would go back on the bus. All my friends from the Center came to visit me too.

Thus, assistance during times of illness is considered the family's or children's primary obligation toward their aged parents. As a side note, aged friends, in general, are not able to fully care for one another because of their own physical condition and fear of becoming ill themselves. Their bodies are not as strong as they once were, and some have difficulty in getting around. However, friends provide emotional support by visiting and calling during a friend's illness.

Maria also referred to notions of familism and how they influence older Chicanas to turn to their children for assistance with health-related matters. Older Chicanas basically expect their children to provide health-related assistance. Again, however, such assistance is conditionally based on their children's economic status and the interpersonal relationships between the aged and their families. Maria told the following story.

> If a person needs help, like not being able to cook, or clean, then they should be given some assistance. But if a person is still in their right mind, it's better they live alone. Because some people don't get along. Just because they're relatives doesn't mean they're always going to get along. I've seen some terrible family fights and I don't want any part of that. Some people take care of their elderly parents because they feel sorry for them or because "you have to have me here by force!" That's *real* hard on both the parents and children. Say when a person is sick and has weak hands, a lot of us begin to lose the full use of our hands. We get clumsy, especially when we drink coffee. When we spill things, people get so upset because we're not supposed to spill things, we're not little kids, but we're getting older. So when we do spill things, our children get so upset because we ruin their rugs or tablecloths, they scold us. If you're alone, you don't have to go through the embarrassment of scoldings. If you live with someone else, you have to worry about offending everyone in the house.

The narrative supports several important points. Maria referred to the reality of family relationships. Simply, some families have positive or good relationships; others do not. Second, Maria said that many children are willing but may feel pressured into caring for their aged parents. Most interesting is her reference to aging with dignity by avoiding public scrutiny for her aged condition.

The social context of family networks is primarily displayed by visiting aged parents. Spending the holidays together, shopping, attending church, going out for dinner are all aspects of social and to some extent emotional support. For example, Berta said "on Sundays, I spend time with my family, we go to church or to the park . . . we go shopping." However, it is primarily daughters who have contact with aged parents, as it is daughters who perform emotional and social labor during an aged parent's illness. It is well-documented that women generally care for parents during illness, visit, shop, and in some instances attend church with aged parents. Men have been known to provide financial rather than emotional and social support.

Visiting is frequent but subject to certain circumstances. Contemporary U.S. family life is not conducive to long hours of random visiting. For example, Concepcíon said, "I do visit my children, but they all have their separate and busy lives. Sometimes I get in the way with their lives. I don't want to get in the way or be a burden."

Besides health-related assistance and social contact, another feature of family networks is financial assistance other than what is provided for health care. The degree to which the aged are dependent on their children for financial assistance, obviously, largely depends on the state of their relationships and whether children have money to give their parents. For example, when I asked Berta if she felt comfortable to ask her son for financial assistance, she responded by saying, "No, why? so I can argue with her!" (she pointed to a picture of her daughter-in-law). Another woman who also has very strained familial relationships said, "not one of my other children visits me. Monica is the only one that visits." Monica regularly visited her mother.

Ysidra hesitated to ask for financial help because she did not want to jeopardize her only good relationship. Speaking of her daughter, she said,

No, she doesn't help me with anything. I don't want to bother her with that. She could help me, she could because she tells me, "Mama, whatever you need." She gives me gifts. Not too long ago, she came over and brought me one of those little television sets, a real little one.

Many aged parents ask for money only when they absolutely need it. Most of the women in my study received some type of financial support from their children when needed. Provisions of financial support through housing assistance proved to be the most contradictory dynamic of the older Chicana's relationship to her children. Many said that their children had offered to give them a place to live in their homes, but most said, "Yes, they've offered, but I don't want to live with them." Of the 30 women interviewed, only one woman lived with a daughter. This woman told me the only reason she does so is personal financial difficulties. Thus, the reality of older Chicanas living alone may be a result of either personal choice or circumstance. All but four of the 30 women who participated in this study lived alone; one woman lived with her daughter, another lived with a female friend, and two were married.

Interestingly, the women were most resistant to receiving this type of support. Antoñia said,

My daughter wanted me to sell the house after I had retired and to live with her, but I said no. "You're settled in your home with your family, your husband." I don't mind being alone. I don't want to be a burden on them. I like being independent. I have my own lifestyle and am settled in my ways.

I'm used to living alone and being on my own. I like getting up and doing what I like to do when I want to do it. I want to live the remainder of my life peacefully and enjoy it the way I want to.

Maria voiced a similar opinion:

You know how the saying goes, "what you don't know won't hurt you." If they have a fight or are having problems, I'm not there to hear or see anything. Here alone in my house, I don't know what's happening with them. It's better for a person to live alone. You can go to the show, the stores, your friends come over, and you enjoy yourself.

Concepcíon said,

When you live alone, you can go to sleep when you want to, get up when you want. . . . When you get hungry, you don't have to go around telling anyone that you're hungry, that you want some coffee, that you want a piece of bread or something like that . . . no, because right away, they start in by saying, "oh what a fussy woman!" . . . oh yes.

These statements show the importance women placed on remaining independent, on being able to live their lives as they chose. The women in this particular study were able to make such choices because they were relatively healthy and had stable incomes, whether or not they were supplemented by their children. In some respects, old age has provided older Chicanas the opportunity to make decisions about their lives. Separate residences may also be a means of maintaining good family relationships. Maintaining good familial relationships, ultimately, is important for older Chicanas as they attempt to redefine their relationship to their children.

Older Chicanas are responding to the objective conditions of their familial relationship with a preoccupation and genuine concern regarding their subjective sense of self in relationship to family. In a very complex fashion, older Chicanas want to maintain a sense of independence from family so that they may define their "public" relationship to the family as an *older* woman, more specifically a cultural teacher. The older Chicana's "private" sense of self is that of being someone's companion, whether or not sex is involved, to not be considered an asexual person.

Older Chicanas are engaging cultural definitions of older women. In essence, they are responding to constraining elements of familism involving women. Older Chicanas are discriminating in accepting assistance, particularly with housing, as they fear becoming a convenient baby-sitter. On the other end of the spectrum, children of older Chicanas look to their aged mothers for child care for economic reasons (to defray child care costs) and for cultural reasons (to instill and reinforce cultural values among their own children). Contradictions of familism surface when we ask why grandmothers, or older women, are expected to provide child care. Children of aged parents have been culturally socialized to regard the older Chicana as *la abuelita* (an affectionate reference to Chicana/Latina grandmothers). La abuelita, however, means an older grandmother who willingly provides child care for her grandchildren. Thus, in part, the economic and cultural dependency on aged parents is justified through familism, or more specifically by the cultural definitions of older Chicanas.

To support these arguments, I refer again to the five composite women, as they explained why older Chicanas, at least in this study, preferred not to live with their children. For example, Concepción said,

People are set in their own ways. My daughter has a different personality than I do. She runs her family the way she wants to. I don't have the right to interfere because that's not my family, but hers. I'd rather live here alone. Sometimes they just think you're a baby-sitter and I don't like that. I didn't raise my grandchildren, but took care of them when I had to.

After 2 years of living with her daughter, Maria decided to live alone. She said she became trapped as a convenient baby-sitter and no longer had time for herself.

I lived with my daughter for 2 years, when they built her house. Anyway I moved because I didn't have time for myself. But I'm close to the children. I'm not dependent on anybody, not financially, but I'm emotionally dependent on my family.

I think emotionally I'm not independent, but financially I'm OK. I love my grandchildren and always want to be with them. I spend the weekends with my daughter to be with them, but I don't want to be there taking care of them all the time.

The desire, or more likely, *el mal necesario* (necessary evil) of living independently is stressed in these comments. Independent living does more than just maintain good familial relationships. The desire to live peaceful lives could be compromised if the older Chicana resided with her family. More important, by living alone, she can *secure* her old-age independence. In other words, if she lives alone, she is less likely to fall impulsively into the caretaker role. Thus many of these women had decided to live independently, even though their financial resources were scarce.

The preceding discussion contributed new information on Chicano aging and family studies. For this older Chicana population, family networks should consist of mutual assistance among all family members. Assistance and support during illness is a major priority and primary responsibility of the aged's children. With more and more people residing in nursing homes, some women feel very insecure about their own immediate futures.[3] Many hope they are not stricken with a debilitating illness, for fear they may be placed in a convalescent hospital or nursing home. Obviously, elderly people do not want to reside in nursing homes. Older Chicanas expect their children to care for them as long as they can. Many believe convalescent hospitals and nursing homes are an alternative that shows lack of responsibility and care on the part of their children. Antoñia summed this up:

> As soon as the mother or father gets sick, they put them in a nursing home so they don't have to bother with them. Did you hear what happened to Marta? That's not *our* way of thinking, no, . . . no. If someone gets sick, everyone should help out, some should come one day, the others on another day. But, [children] should take care of [their parents] in their home, not in a nursing home. I think a person dies sooner [in a nursing home] because they don't take care of you, they don't pay attention to you in there.

During my 2-year tenure with these women, only one woman was stricken with a debilitating illness, a stroke. Marta was the mother of five children, all well-educated and securely employed. Marta's children decided to place their mother in a nursing home because she needed professional health care around the clock. All her children were in dual wage-earning families. Having someone leave the labor force, most likely a daughter or daughter-in-law, would have involved a financial risk for that caretaker's family. Also, all of Marta's children, with the exception of one, had children of their own. The aged community viewed this decision by Marta's children as disrespectful, irresponsible, and uncaring. Many times, aged parents have difficulty understanding and accepting when families place them in convalescent or nursing homes. I am not advocating that older people, because of financial security, be conveniently placed in health care facilities. Families must take many factors into consideration before major decisions are made with respect to caring for aged parents.

Obviously, not all families make similar decisions. In many families, a member, usually a daughter or other female relative, leaves the labor force to care for an ill, aged parent. Granted this is not an easy decision for families to make. However, for Chicano families such decisions are further complicated by assessing one's financial status in light of one's family obligation or the ideological force of familism. Thus, many Chicano families find themselves in a contradictory situation in attempting to make sound decisions for their parents and paying attention to their own economic situation, while also soothing any sense of guilt they may have for placing their parent in a nursing home.

Nonetheless, as more and more Chicano elderly live into old age, long-term care will be a vital health care issue for the Chicano population. To what extent cultural values interact with economic status will be a very crucial question in the very near future for Chicano families with aged parents.

The evidence suggests that familial networks among the aged no longer constitute the "romanticized" extended family so often described in Chicano aging literature. Historically, the family may have provided all levels of support for the aged. In this study, women tended to live alone, many by choice, others by circumstance. Most of these women had chosen to live alone mainly to protect their independence from threats by the responsibility of child care.

Older Chicanas are faced with cultural constraints that define old age in the traditional context of caretaker. The family network provides a sense of security within a context of obligation. Older Chicanas stand somewhat assured that children and grandchildren will assist in times of illness and provide financial need when necessary. However, there is no indication that the familial network structure provides a definite role and status for these women. To clarify, previous literature concluded that aged parents had definite roles and statuses in the family hierarchy. Basically, grandmothers were considered caregivers. Questions may surface as to whether the lack of the traditional grandmother role creates psychological anxiety or a sense of displacement for older Chicanas. I argue that they do not experience a sense of discontinuity with respect to this role. However, because they no longer have a definite role in the family, they may experience some isolation. Such an argument assumes that older Chicanas only see themselves as grandmothers. Their sense of womanhood is subsumed within this expectation.

Within the objective complexities of the family relationship, I found these women to have a strong desire to remain independent, while adhering to certain traditions. They agreed that the family was important and should provide assistance for all family members. However, they had very strong convictions regarding their personal interests. As older women, they wanted to determine their old age independently, outside the expectations associated with grandmotherhood.

Hence, the familial network does not provide older Chicanas an opportunity to deal with themselves as older women. The familial network may provide security, respect, and the role of grandmother. However, their sense of self as older women is not recognized within familial networks.

In some sense, these women were redefining family relationships with respect to their participation in familial networks. It was evident from the data that they did not see themselves solely as caregivers. Older Chicanas continued to value familial obligation and assistance among all family members, especially in times of need. In particular, older Chicanas expected their children to care for them during illness. As mentioned earlier, putting relatives in convalescent homes was viewed as displaying a lack of respect, care, and responsibility.

The independence these women wanted to maintain allowed them to redefine themselves with respect to the family. The family wants a traditional, asexual grandmother. Older Chicanas want to be grandmothers but not exploited grandmothers; they also want to establish themselves as cultural teachers and older women who are not asexual. The process involved in establishing their subjective sense of self is the focus of the following chapter.

NOTES

1. An early study of informal supports found that Latino elderly had consistently higher levels of interaction and a greater potential for support from children than did either white or African American elderly, even controlling for gender, social class, and level of functional ability (Cantor, 1979). Older Latinos were more likely than Anglos to believe that older persons should be cared for in the community, and they were more than four times as likely as Anglos between the ages of 65 and 74, and more than two times as likely as those 74 years of age and older, to live with their adult children. Widowed women over 75 were the most likely to live in extended family households (Cuellar, 1990).

2. Nearly 50% of older women (compared to 16% of older men) lived alone for about one third of their adult lives, primarily because of widowhood or divorce. In 1890, widows lived alone for 5 to 10 years; now, the average is 24 years alone, and at the same time, fewer adult children are available to provide care (Huckle, 1991).

3. Only about 3% of Latino elderly are in nursing homes, including 10% of those over 85 compared with 23% of Anglos of this age (Cuellar, 1990). We must be cautious of these statistics as they refer to those over 85. Economic, cultural, and life expectancy factors should be taken into consideration when considering these statistics. Some researchers speculate that with higher incomes among the Latino aged's children, the possibility of being placed in a convalescent home increases. See Markides, Martin, and Gomez, 1983, Chapters 5-6.

5

Being an Older Woman Means Being More Than Just a Grandma

The older Chicana's attempt to redefine her womanhood conflicts with cultural expectations of older women's lives. For older Chicanas who are grandmothers or *abuelas,* Chicano culture imposes the traditional role of caregiving. This chapter focuses on the older Chicana's hopes for expanding her role to that of a cultural teacher within the family and subsequently the larger Chicano community.

Pesquera (1985) and Segura (1986) said that motherhood and male authority were elements of Chicano family ideology or familism. Male authority or patriarchy relegates women to roles as mothers. Turning to familism as an ideology would help redefine the study of older Chicanas in broader sociological terms. In other words, it is important to look to ideology to understand where familism is rooted with respect to class, race/ethnicity, gender, and culture. To do this, we must identify the ideological components associated with familism and older Chicanas.

My findings refute the empirical evidence in Chicano aging literature. First, let us refer to the notion of the multigenerational household or extended family. In the lives of my respondents, familism as an empirical phenomenon, or manifestations of expected mutual aid and support, appears to have modified, while certain elements of familism, namely family unity, have remained.

In other words, the multigenerational household and extended family do not operate as the literature would lead us to believe. My findings suggest older Chicanas have established modified definitions and control for women. Certain values, caregiving in particular, continue to be imposed with transitions to grandmotherhood. Because of their sex and age,

Chicana grandmothers are expected to continue in a caregiver role. This constitutes a continued reproduction of gender throughout the life course for the women in this study.

Hence, I am concerned with *cultural expectations* placed on older women who are grandmothers, not the familial or community roles for which many older Chicanas are recognized. For example, Espin (1992) said "that middle-aged and elderly Hispanic women retain important roles in their families even after their sons and daughters are married" (p. 142). Generally, opinions and advice of older Chicanas or grandmothers are sought in major family decisions, thus rendering these women integral members in family affairs. Some may also act as providers of mental health services in an unofficial way as *curanderas* "for those people who believe in these alternative approaches to health care" (Espin, p. 142). Also, some Chicana grandmothers have knowledge of herbal remedies for physical ailments. Some of these women can play a powerful role in their communities, given their reputation for being able to heal mind and body. Espin further argued that older Latina women may have more status and power than their Anglo counterparts. However, unlike the role of caregiver, these roles are not culturally prescribed.

As older Chicanas attempt to define and resolve their womanhood, they question and challenge cultural expectations, at the risk of being disrespected. Capitalizing on this respect is critical as this facilitates the process of defining her womanhood. The family simultaneously presents a means of support, love, and respect, while stressing conformity and ultimately control. The older Chicana's self-aspiration as a cultural teacher threatens to alter tradition as cultural expectations imposed on older Chicanas are antithetical to her desired existence.

To begin the examination of this dialectic, our discussion focuses on grandmotherhood. Based on the data collected, *grandmotherhood* can be defined as a stage in the life course when women, based on their age and sex, are expected to primarily conform to a caregiving and nurturing role. Thus, grandmotherhood essentially involves "grandmothering," where older Chicanas provide care and nurture for grandchild(ren) and/or great-grandchild(ren). In general, older Chicanas welcome grandmotherhood, at the same time they hope to redefine and broaden their relationship to the family. Chicana grandmothers are willing to assist with child care when necessary. But they object to the idea of grandmothers as convenient "baby-sitters." An important issue these women clarified was the distinction between "raising" *(crear)* grandchildren, and providing "child care" *(quidar)*. For example, Concepcíon said: "I didn't raise my grandchildren, but took care of them when I had to."

Experiences of grandmotherhood are no doubt varied. Generally, women in this study were satisfied with their relationships to their children and grandchildren. However, it is clear they did not see themselves solely as caregivers. For example, Maria said,

> I love it, but I'm not the kind of grandma where I'm going to sit down and only knit little things for my grandkids or nothing. They come here and they know my rules. As a matter of fact, the 5-year-old comes here. She comes with her little bag of clothes, to change and everything, and says, "Yes, yes, I know grandma, this is your house, and we have to do what you tell us to do and you're not afraid of my father, so if I've been bad, you're going to spank me." And I demand respect. Some of my grandkids don't speak Spanish, but I teach them to say abuela, not grandma.

Not all grandmothers have positive familial relationships, as the literature would lead us to believe. A few women have little or no contact with their grandchildren because of geographical distance or poor familial relationships.

Chicana grandmothers do not feel obligated to provide child care, although in times of need, they provide care for their grandchildren and great-grandchildren. Many women said they wanted to use the independence that old age has brought them in ways other than caregiving. For many, this is the first time they have had the opportunity to define or construct their own lives, without the responsibility of caring for a parent, spouse, or children. Antoñia described her expectations and obligations as a Chicana grandmother:

> I thought that if I'm gonna be a grandma I could help mi'ja when she needed my help, but I was not obligated to stay home and take care of her children so she could have a good time . . . no oh no . . . because the grandparents have the right to be free and enjoy themselves when they're old or young or whatever. You have to have some consideration for your parents, not load them with children because they're grandparents or they're old. If she has to work, but not take care of them every day, no.

Berta also spoke on the subject of women being regarded exclusively as child care providers.

I don't think the grandma should be just the baby-sitter. No, not me. I love it. But like I say, you know, when they need help yes, but not because they want to go out or something. If it's a special occasion, OK, like an anniversary or Mother's Day. I feel like it's not my obligation to raise their kids. I can help in case of sickness or something but not as a place where everybody can dump their kids and have a good time or because I'm the grandma.

Mercedes confirmed Berta's sentiments and objections:

Oh no, not that. I think that grandmothers, with married children, if they can help out from time to time, OK. But to be here struggling with my grandkids, no more. I already raised my kids, no more. I like to go shopping, to the show, once in a while to a restaurant. My grandchildren don't hold me back from enjoying myself. I'm already a great-grandmother, it's time for me to rest. After eight kids, oh no!

Beyond the desire to establish themselves as cultural teachers, these women are no doubt influenced by their age. Many of these women are great-grandmothers and no longer have the energy to care for grandchildren or great-grandchildren. With their first grandchild they were elated. In many cases, these women admitted to wanting to have the grandchild daily. But they have very strong feelings about the obligations of grandmothers. One of these obligations is not baby-sitting.

According to the older women in this study, grandmotherhood should not mean an obligation to perform tasks associated with mothering: caregiving and nurturing. If the caregiver role is culturally valued, caregiving and nurturing should be regarded as the abuela's contribution to mutual forms of assistance within familial networks. However, given the existence of patriarchy, caregiving and nurturing are not valued in society, thus contributing to women's oppression. Because of traditional socialization with respect to female/male roles, older Chicanas are accepting of the caregiver role when it is respected and not taken for granted, thus continuing to define grandmotherhood within a traditional context. I am not arguing that grandmotherhood should be defined in relationship to a traditional role of caregiving. On the contrary, I am attempting to illuminate how grandmotherhood is regarded within the Chicano community and among older Chicanas. Hence, grandmotherhood defined within this context warrants respect, under the condition that older women conform to the cultural expectation of caregiver. Thus, grandmotherhood as defined contributes to a status of both power and powerlessness.

As illustrated in the data, the element of powerlessness lies in the potential exploitation of older Chicanas as convenient caregivers or baby-sitters. Generally, grandmothering is a difficult task. However, of greater concern is the limited view of older women simply as caregivers. The process of establishing oneself as a cultural teacher involves retaining and capitalizing on respect granted to older women who conform to the caregiver role. The conditions under which older women attempt to capitalize on respect differ for widowed and married grandmothers.

Of the 30 women interviewed, 26 were widowed grandmothers, 2 were married grandmothers, and 2 never had children. For the widowed grandmother to retain respect, she must remain single and refrain from seeking male companionship. The widowed grandmother is expected to respect the memory of her past marriage by remaining widowed and conforming to a traditional role of caregiver. Older widowed grandmothers are discouraged from seeking male companionship. This proscription ultimately controls their sexuality, whether in fact they seek companionship. Thus, the abuela, like most aged persons, is considered asexual. Even though companionship among older people may not necessarily be sexual, older Chicanas do have a sense of sexuality. Cultural expectations, ageism, and patriarchy define and subsequently influence the expression of older Chicana sexuality.

Older widowed grandmothers who challenge this expectation risk being judged as a "bad" woman or *una mujer sin verguenza*. The dichotomy of the "good" versus "bad" woman serves to ensure that aged widowed grandmothers will commit themselves to cultural expectations of caregiving. If widowed grandmothers do not concede to this cultural expectation, they risk losing the respect needed to establish themselves as cultural teachers.

According to Espin (1992), "the honor of Latin families is strongly tied to the sexual purity of women" (p. 142). The idea of the virgin/whore dichotomy stems from Catholicism. Again, referring to Espin, "the Virgin Mary, who was a virgin and a mother, but never a sexual being, is considered an important role model for Hispanic women" (p. 142). Young women are encouraged to remain virgins until marriage, and older women are encouraged to be celibate after marriage. Thus, the implication is that women should engage in sex only to procreate and should shun sexual pleasure.

Married grandmothers are not bound by the restriction. It is assumed they will not seek male companionship. Therefore, their aspirations as cultural teachers should not be hindered. However, they are still expected to conform to the traditional caregiving role. Only two women in this study were not biological grandmothers. One woman was a surrogate grandmother to her goddaughter's children. The other woman married late in life and did not have any children of her own. She too acted as a surrogate "grandmother" to her younger sibling's children. Given that they were widows, they also were discouraged from seeking male companionship. These women were expected to retain a sense of respect among their immediate families and the larger Chicano community by remaining single.

Older women's children, and the community in general, tend to regard Chicana grandmothers as ready, willing, and able to provide child care. What is important to clarify is that caregiving carries no guarantee of respect. Being caregivers does not necessarily earn women the respect they need to become cultural teachers. If an aged grandmother does seek male companionship, she may not be granted the respect needed to become a cultural teacher. However, having male companionship in no way bars her children and, in some cases, grandchildren, from seeking her services as a caregiver. Grandmothering is viewed as culturally valid. Seeking male companionship is culturally disrespectful.

Antoñia had been living alone for nearly 20 years. Because of the expectations that are held about older Chicano women, Antoñia had difficulty addressing the issue of companionship. During the interview, many of the women waited for a comfortable moment to share their thoughts and feelings about this issue. I asked Antoñia if the Chicano community treated women differently once they became widowed. She began by saying she did not know. Initially, this was a way of avoiding conversations about companionship.

She began by rationalizing why some older women may seek companionship. She stated that many women have had "hard lives." By this she meant many women were physically, emotionally, and/or psychologically abused in their marriages. According to Antoñia, once these women become widows, they now "feel free" and are anxious to have a "good" relationship with someone. Second, she adopted the Chicano community's cultural norms by adamantly telling me not to repeat the story of her friend, Carmen. The following is Antoñia's account of Carmen's experience.

I haven't seen, but I've heard that a lot of men treat their wives really bad. When they die, well, a woman feels free. So they're anxious to marry whoever not thinking that it might not be good, they just think it'll be better, but sometimes the second is worse than the first. That's what I've heard [long pause] . . . that's what's happening to my friend, Carmen. Don't say anything! There's a man who's courting her, but don't you say anything to anyone!

Concepcíon Villegas had been widowed for 14 years and lived alone. She addressed the expectations placed on the older Chicana widow, focusing in particular on how women who seek male companionship run the risk of being categorized as either good or bad. This categorization perpetuates a traditional relationship to the older woman's family. Concepcíon said,

When I became a widow, if you talk to men, they think you are bad, that you talk to them and want them to have maybe an affair, become a sweetheart or whatever, and that's when I changed because I couldn't talk to my friends or to a man like friendly, or other words the way I am because I like to talk to everybody and I don't like to distinguish anyone, see, but when I became a widow I didn't want them to think because I need their company or whatever [she laughs] no.

Mercedes had been widowed for 10 years and, she too, lived alone. Mercedes was the most comfortable and adamant in addressing the issue of companionship. She said,

Well, there's a lot of women . . . well, when their husbands pass away they begin to have a lot of friends, both men and women, and they go out and all that. Sometimes that can be good, and other times it isn't when other people see you and they begin to talk. They'll say, "Look at the way she's acting now, before don't you remember what a saint! . . . Now look what's happening, that woman's up to no good." That's the first thing that people say! They don't say, "she's trying to enjoy herself because she needs to get out, she needs to keep herself busy, she needs to keep preoccupied." They don't say that, they say just the opposite. That's the problem that a lot of women have, I've seen it with my own eyes, and I've heard it from other people.

Berta, who was married, also expressed her opinions: "I say that widowed women have to be careful how they handle themselves so that people around them will respect them, because if you don't act in a respectable manner, they will never respect you in any way."

Finally, Maria shared her experiences of how the community and particularly her children reacted to her companionship. Maria Gonzales had been widowed for 10 years and lived with her 30-year-old daughter.

> Well, I'm gonna tell you something. They criticized me when I used to go with this man. This man used to go to the Center, that's where I met him, and I never paid attention to him. He told me himself that he was watching me for a month or more than a month, but I never paid attention to him. I never talked to him until they had a dance to celebrate the birthdays. He took me out to dance and he liked the way I dance, so we became friends. There were many people that criticized us because we were together. And my children said I was too old to have a friend. Your kids think that once you're old, you're dead or something. They get very jealous. And the first thing they say is "what about my father?" Well, what about their father, he's dead, may he rest in peace, but I'm not! See, if you're a widow, they want you to stay home, be a good little grandma. Yes, we can go out, but don't uh . . . don't try to make friends with men. It's hard to be a widow.

Generally the community, but particularly children of older Chicanas, hold strong objections to their mother's involvement with men. Some children threaten to withhold financial support. Others discontinue regular visits and phone calls. And still others display their discontent by playing on their mother's guilt for not respecting their father's memory.

Given the constraints imposed on the older Chicana's womanhood, how then do these women remain respected while challenging cultural expectations? As illustrated in the preceding discussion, Chicana grandmothers are altering the traditional role of caregiving. Chicana grandmothers will provide child care out of necessity but not for convenience sake. This, in turn, grants them independence and leverage in defining their relationship to the family. Under these conditions, child care services are viewed as an important form of mutual aid to the family. The attempt, on the part of older Chicanas, is to socially construct the caregiver role as an important form of familial support rather than a form of control. Nonetheless, their womanhood, with respect to grandmothering, continues to be defined within a traditional context.

The process of socially constructing Chicana old age also involves capitalizing on symbolic respect for the aged. Symbolic respect refers to acknowledgment of a specific age hierarchy, which is largely manifested through language. Younger generations are expected to acknowledge the presence of older Chicanos, not render them invisible. They are taught to respect the aged for their wisdom and knowledge, for their survival into old age.

With respect to language use, symbolic respect dictates the tone in which younger generations address and communicate with the aged. Many aged Chicanos who are either grandmothers or grandfathers prefer to be addressed in Spanish as *abuela* or *abuelo* or the endearing terms of *abuelita* or *abuelito*. Unrelated aged individuals prefer to be addressed as *señora, señor,* and in few cases, *doña or don*. Also, the form *usted* as opposed to *tu* is emphasized when addressing elders.

Older Chicanas' quest to redefine their womanhood obviously depends on their relationship to their children. However, given the cultural prerequisite of respect for the aged, older Chicanas are placed in an advantageous situation. This enables them to maintain contact with their children and, most important, grandchildren and for some great-grandchildren. Such contact, whether through visits, social gatherings, or caregiving services, allows for older Chicanas to establish themselves as cultural teachers and subsequently to redefine womanhood, while maintaining positive familial relationships.

The challenge for the two married grandmothers in the study was to maintain positive familial relationships, thus capitalizing on symbolic respect for the aged. Widowed grandmothers who try to reconstruct old age may violate cultural norms related to female sexuality. For the remaining 28 widowed grandmothers, living alone, involvement with senior centers and/or the church, and friendship networks are additional resources that contribute to an identity independent from the family. As older Chicanas' involvement in such environments grows, they move from a dependent to interdependent relationship with their families, thus providing them with more leverage in negotiating and resolving their womanhood.

As cultural teachers, older Chicanas want to socialize grandchild(ren) and/or great-grandchild(ren) with certain cultural values and traditions, particularly their behavior toward older people and the maintenance of Spanish. The preservation of music, food, and, for some, religion, is viewed as equally important. Given their socioeconomic status, older Chicanas are placed in a position where they can leave a legacy of cultural rather than monetary value. For example, Mercedes said,

I would like to tell my grandchildren what children used to be like, how a child used to behave. I think we should tell them through stories. When older people come over, they should greet them, and speak politely to them. They should also respect when older people want to talk among themselves.

Mercedes also spoke of the rich oral tradition of storytelling in Chicano culture. Concepcíon discussed the Spanish language.

I would like for all my grandchildren to speak Spanish. I have some grandchildren who speak Spanish and others who don't. I'm not trying to take their English away because I know real well that they need it. But their parents have to teach them too, that's how I feel. I would like for my grandchildren to speak both languages.

CONCLUSION

The social construction of womanhood for older Chicanas involves reconceptualizing the traditional expectation of caregiving and the role of cultural teacher. In altering rather than dismantling the caregiving role, older Chicanas continue to define their womanhood within a traditional context. Generally, they continue to view themselves as grandmothers who are both caregivers and nurturers. Hence, reconceptualization involves the way in which the caregiver role is regarded among the Chicano community. At present, cultural expectations, and the conditions under which older Chicanas are pressured to conform as caregivers, serve as mechanisms of social control. For older Chicanas, the caregiver role should be valued and respected as an important form of financial and social support.

As cultural teachers, older Chicanas are recognized as people of knowledge and wisdom. Most important, they act as carriers of the cultural legacy, thus playing an important part in preserving culture. Interestingly, in providing child care, older Chicanas are more likely than men to have contact with their families, allowing for the role of cultural teacher to develop. This is not to say that one cannot establish oneself as a cultural teacher outside of a child care context or that men cannot establish themselves as cultural teachers. The point is that women have effectively used their limited resources in socially constructing their womanhood, namely their family and their relationships to the family.

In moving toward definitions of womanhood among older Chicanas, the concept *abuela* or grandmother merits attention. The term abuela connotes a romanticized image of older Chicanas that only serves to disempower women within their families and among the community. It is interesting to note that when older Chicanas are discussed in the literature, they are almost always referred to as grandmothers. Thus, the terms grandmother and older woman are synonymous.

For older Chicanas, grandmotherhood should be a status of respect, not only because of their age and their potential as caregivers. Grandmotherhood should bring recognition for their position in the family, their labor as caregivers and nurturers, and their contributions to familial support systems. Older Chicanas desire an age hierarchy that would recognize them not only as grandmothers, but also as cultural teachers and older women who are not necessarily asexual.

6

Conclusion

I've done what I've had to do . . . but, I don't feel useless. It's a different
life now. . . . I have the Center, my friends, my grandchildren, and my
garden.

Concepcíon, 76

This study has used ethnographic methods to explore the complexity of
old age among older Chicanas. This group of older Chicanas expected
old age to bring solace, harmony, respect, and status. The family would
continue to shield the aged from the outside "hostile" world. Children
and grandchildren would provide financial, emotional, and social support. Consequently, the aged would feel secure, and their place in both
the family and society would be well-defined and recognized. Older Chicanas, in general, were not socialized to fear old age but to welcome the
reality of growing old.

Coupled with these expectations are images of themselves as older
women. The image of older Chicanas has been that of grandmother, cultural teacher, and giver of advice. Grandmotherhood meant assisting with
child care, and in some cases, raising grandchildren. As cultural teachers,
Chicanas were expected to educate younger family members, in particular grandchildren, about cultural traditions and values, for example, food,
music, Catholicism, and the Spanish language. Finally, with old age
came wisdom and knowledge. Older Chicanas were "matriarchs" providing advice about family matters such as marriage, parenting, and health
care.

The reality of older Chicana lives, however, has clashed with these
expectations and images. Nearly all the women in this study have had to

deal with two major relocations, the move from Mexico to the United States and from rural to urban areas. These transitions have had major implications for their aging experiences. The inner world of aging, from their perspective, consists of changing familial structures and threatened cultural values. There are no underpinnings in dealing with the changing context of old age. There are no traditional ways of confronting poverty and isolation outside the family. Ultimately the aged only have one another to look to for guidance. Thus, developing strategies for challenging old age has resulted in modified expectations of being old.

Old age for these women means being poor, living alone, and being pressured by a life-long career of caregiving. Monthly incomes barely exceed living expenses, keeping older Chicanas living on the brink of poverty. Many live in impoverished neighborhoods, making them more socially vulnerable because they are older Chicanas.

Family relationships are complex and determined by personal, economic, and social factors. Society, in general, is no longer conducive to the multigenerational households in which older Chicanas were reared. On the one hand, many elderly desire to live alone, even though their resources are limited. On the other, children are geographically distant primarily because of jobs and school.

Perceptions of older Chicanas have been clouded with romanticized images of *la abuelita* (grandmother). Cultural values rooted in gender have caused older Chicanas to be identified primarily as grandmothers. In addition, grandmothers were considered a part of the family. Grandmotherhood was expected to be her primary role, as well as her last. With changing family structures, traditional grandmotherhood is being challenged. Older Chicanas have responded to familial changes, poverty, and isolation by drawing on their limited resources, namely the family and, for some, voluntary organizations. In turn, older Chicanas have attempted to constructively determine their old age. Ironically, old age has brought a new-found independence, which has allowed older Chicanas to define their sense of womanhood.

Given these changes and contradictions, how have they come to understand old age? What is important now in their lives? Like most elderly, they worry about their health, money, and their families. With respect to health, however, they fear being an invalid more than they fear dying. Much of this fear is alleviated by their beliefs in Catholicism. As one woman stated,

I'm not afraid to die, when my time comes, it comes . . . the only thing that makes me think, if I have a long sickness and I'm an invalid or something, I don't know if there's gonna be somebody to take care of me.

Old age for Chicanas means more than simply being content or depressed. Obviously, life is difficult. Nearly all the women in this study stated they were content, satisfied with their children, and grateful they have lived to be old. As one woman said,

I'm not depressed because I'm old. No, absolutely not, because my kids are all grown. I don't have to worry about anyone. I've lived my life. I raised my kids, I educated them and everything. Now it's up to them to take care of themselves, they don't need me anymore, to cook, to clean. Now, I'm free, I'm free now, if I want to go to the Center, I go. If I don't want to go, I don't go. I'm not missed any more in the house. I'm no longer needed. You see, I'm alone, but I'm happy. I'm happy I got the chance to live this long.

Another woman said,

I'm really happy I had the opportunity to have a good marriage and educate my kids. All I ever wanted was to educate my kids. I lived for that. Staying up with them all hours of the night when they were studying . . . taking them coffee, apples, so they wouldn't fall asleep . . . with all of them. Now it scares me that I had so much energy, how did I do that? Carrots and oranges . . . it was a lot of work.

Berta expressed her feelings about old age in these terms:

Old people shouldn't feel useless because they're old. No, I feel content because I'm enjoying my old age. I've lived my life and I'm happy that I can live as an older person. When you're old, you can't look at life with sadness . . . you're not as strong or healthy as you are when you're young. When you're old you have to take care of yourself. But I know I have to live with these sicknesses. I thank God He let me live this long and I appreciate it and enjoy it. You have to appreciate your old age as you are.

Old age is accepted, but not challenged. The conditions of old age are much more difficult than the state of being old. Given their attitudes toward being old, death is not feared. Many women said that although people obviously do not want to die, death is "the other side of the coin." Some said that being old was a time to rest, "a time to patiently wait for death." As one woman said, "We have to accept death like we do life. I don't worry about dying because our lives are in the hands of God. I just want to go to Mexico one more time before I die."

This study has provided an analysis of Chicana old age beyond the concept of familism by examining the older Chicana experience in broader sociological terms. Chicano aging research has focused primarily on the interrelationship of aging and the concept of familism. The approach has been widely accepted and is a primary guiding framework in Chicano aging studies. Familism has been used as an all-encompassing concept for explaining the complexities of old age. The concept, however, is limited, as it perpetuates traditional images of family life. The family is viewed as the aged's primary source of status and social support. In particular, older women are portrayed primarily as caregivers, or abuelas. Closer examination of this approach reveals that familism is largely rooted in the social construct of gender. Thus the concept of familism obscures the realities of Chicana old age. An integrative approach to Chicana aging guided this research. The complex interplay of age, familism, and gender provided the basis for a broader sociological understanding of older lives.

Previous studies on Chicana aging have silenced the voices of older women by assuming their lives were solely engaged with grandmotherhood. Participant observation and analyses of life histories among 30 older Chicanas revealed a sharp contrast to the existing literature. Understanding Chicana aging from their own personal reflections illuminated experiences that are richly diverse.

Unlike previous research, this study portrayed older Chicanas as actively determining their old age. Older Chicanas used community resources such as senior citizen centers to deal with the discontinuities of old age. The Center allowed the elderly to develop a sense of self-worth, a positive identity as old people. Because the elderly are invisible to the outside world, the Center compensated for lost identities and statuses. The Center was constructed as a place where the aged could appear, be seen, act, interact, and exist.

Older Chicanas established their self-worth through activities and organized groups. The activities women engaged in at the Center reflected the division of labor that characterized their marriages and work experiences. Gender-specific tasks such as crocheting, preparing meals, and maintaining the household were extended from the home and performed in the Center. In addition, the women perpetuated the importance of Catholicism, a responsibility passed on to Chicanas by their mothers and grandmothers. Hence older Chicanas as a group were more complex and active than older Chicanos.

Older Chicanas established distinct groups based on the above-mentioned gender-specific activities. These groups were markers of existence and self-worth. Hence older Chicanas were able to create a distinct sense of continuity in the aging process. This continuity is attributed to the interaction of age and gender. Old age prescribes activities associated with the private sphere. Older people are expected to "spend their time socializing, taking care of themselves, passing the days pleasantly, and attending to the quality of life and interpersonal concern" (Myerhoff, 1978/1994, p. 262). For older men, this is difficult because of their limited experience with the private sphere. Therefore, older Chicanas have an advantage over men in that their responsibilities associated with the home remain viable in old age.

On the one hand, patriarchy constrained women to the private sphere. The tasks associated with the home remained viable in old age, allowing older Chicanas to exert vitality and dominance within the Center. However, patriarchy has historically relegated women to low-paying jobs, thus placing them in poverty in old age. Gender becomes contradictory in nature during old age by generating both positive and negative conditions for older Chicanas. The nature of old age as it is defined today has allowed older Chicanas to maintain continuity in the life course.

Finally, the Center provided an arena where aspects of Chicano culture were expressed and reinforced. Physical aspects such as food, music, and language were maintained. Traditional Mexican celebrations such as Cinco de Mayo (Fifth of May), 16th of September, and All Souls Day were acknowledged. Ideologically, the traditional age hierarchy and the notion of *respeto* (respect) were reaffirmed. Because these values found less confirmation in everyday life outside the Center, older Chicanos reaffirmed these values by adhering to interactions and behaviors associated with these values.

Poverty and grandmotherhood contributed to the social construction of Chicana old age. Poverty is largely attributed to a division of labor based on gender. Of the 30 women interviewed, 12 had been widowed within the last 10 years. For these women, old age involved learning to take sole responsibility for their personal and economic welfare. Sustaining adequate incomes exacerbated their disadvantaged socioeconomic situation with the onset of widowhood. With no prior work skills to fall back on,

their economic situation worsened. Older Chicana widows with no previous work experience are not guaranteed social security benefits in old
age. Many are dependent on their husband's minimal pensions or Supplemental Security Income (SSI).

Also, these women were involved in traditional marriages where
women are allocated child care responsibilities and household maintenance. They did not work outside the home. Consequently, dependency
on their husbands developed and continued throughout their marriages
until widowhood. Thus marriages arranged by a division of labor based
on gender creates conditions that make widowhood a difficult social transition and exacerbate poverty in old age.

The remaining 16 older Chicanas, unpartnered widows, were actually
widowed after marital separation or divorce. Nonetheless, they referred
to themselves as widows in order to avoid the stigma associated with
separated and divorced women and to claim an identity and position
among their cohort. Unlike late widows, they did not go through the
transition to widowhood as part of their aging experience. Marital dissolution left these women with young children living in poverty. These
women were forced into the labor market as primary wage earners for the
first time in their lives. Because these women were employed in jobs
segregated by race/ethnicity and gender—factory work, domestics, farm
work, cannery work—they were not entitled to social security benefits.
Consequently, they too are dependent on SSI. A strict division of labor
based on gender that operates in both the home and labor market has
largely shaped poverty among older Chicanas.

Poverty for this population is characterized with an extreme vulnerability to poor health. Given their concerns with debilitating illnesses and
becoming dependent on children, older Chicanas develop a complex relationship with their children for both economic and cultural reasons.
Given the older Chicana's vulnerability to poor health and limited resources, her options are limited in socially constructing old age. Because
of the interdependent relationship between older Chicanas and their children, it is within the context of the familial relationships that the social
construction or definition of Chicana old age beyond the traditional role
of abuela or grandmother takes place.

In addition to the structural constraints of poverty, old age for Chicanas is also shaped by cultural expectations. In general, all cultures pre-
scribe norms and behaviors associated with old age. Chicano culture prescribes that older Chicana widows respect the memory of their marriages
by remaining alone, but content. Among the aged community, seeking
companionship is considered a male privilege. Because of their age,

older Chicanas are also expected to conform to the traditional role of caregiver, otherwise defined in the context of *la abuela*. I argued that the older Chicana's sense of herself as an older woman becomes distorted within these traditions, which impose control based on her age and sex. These cultural expectations contribute to the ideology of Chicana widows as living humbly, alone, and content with grandmotherhood. Ultimately, these expectations or definitions of old age for Chicanas serve as a mechanism of control.

Older Chicanas claimed old age brought a newfound independence that allowed them to determine their old age. Older Chicanas welcomed this independence and sought ways to secure this opportunity. Given their limited resources, determining and establishing their older lives appeared problematic. However, older Chicanas redefined their relationships to the family, especially with respect to their role as caregivers. Older Chicanas did not view their assistance to the familial network in terms of caregiving. One way of avoiding caregiving responsibilities was to live alone. Hence, older Chicanas defined their relationship to the family on more equal or reciprocal terms, as a means of securing their independence in defining their old age beyond that of a caregiver, namely as a cultural teacher.

Chicano culture defines woman's old age in such a way that it is a mechanism of social control. This ensures that older Chicanas will acquiesce to grandmotherhood. Companionship among widowed grandmothers would threaten the availability of the aged woman to provide child care services for her children when needed. Second, in having companionship, she may be negatively regarded and thus not gain the respect, or symbolic respect, she needs in order to establish herself as cultural teacher. In challenging these constraints or cultural norms, she confronts this controlling element, which basically guarantees grandmotherhood. Also, she challenges the assumption of older women as being asexual. Defining oneself as a cultural teacher, an older woman of knowledge and wisdom, essentially reinforces cultural values of symbolic respect.

Finally, the analytical approach used to understand the complexity of old age among Chicanas involves them as speaking subjects. This involves listening to descriptions of aging and old age from women of Mexican descent. Such an approach provides a medium of communication for voices that have been overlooked and unheard inside the walls of academia.

Also, this work was guided by several principles now being addressed in studies of older people (Andersen & Collins, 1994; Stanfield & Dennis, 1993; Stoller & Gibson, 1994). The concepts gender, race/ethnicity, and class were conceptualized as social constructs rather than individual attributes that must be controlled statistically or experimentally (Jackson, 1985). These social constructs are based on social values that influence opportunity structures, adaptive resources, and identity formation. Second, the "social problems" approach implicit in the multiple jeopardy perspective on class, race, and gender was challenged by emphasizing strengths as well as deficits. This study illuminated older Chicanas as active creators of culture rather than simply passive victims. Older women created meaning in their lives despite barriers based on class, race/ethnicity, and gender. We are not only able to understand how older Chicanas negotiate systems of oppression but how they creatively maintain personal integrity in socially constructing old age.

The major theoretical interpretation of this study provides an understanding of how familism and gender simultaneously shape the aging experience for Chicanas. The dialectic of how older Chicanas resolve their sense of old age was a major point of discussion. The family simultaneously represents a means of support, love, and respect while stressing conformity, and ultimately control by imposing the tradition role of abuela, or caregiver. Their aspirations to become cultural teachers threaten to alter tradition, as cultural expectations imposed on older Chicanas are antithetical to their desired existence.

In sum, a partial agenda of the New Aging Period calls for younger generations of Chicanos to critically acknowledge economic and social changes that shape the conditions under which older Chicanas live and their subsequent construction of old age. Failing to do so hinders the liberation of older Chicanas and contributes to their subordination. We can contribute to their liberation by acknowledging the contributions they make regardless of how they choose to define their sexuality. To simply claim that tradition is being attacked, in this case our images of la abuela, is to perpetuate older woman's oppression. Thus, we must move beyond "colonial eyes" and take responsibility for oppressive forces toward women, both in the larger society and within the Chicano community.

With respect to public policy, we are at the crossroads; our challenge is to go beyond being knowledgeable about the experiences of people of different genders, races/ethnicities, and social classes. Policies and programs must be reconsidered as diversity in attitudes, behavior, and resources among older people increases. Simply, but most difficult, public policy must reflect values of fairness and justice, or human rights as opposed to civil rights. On a final note, it is my hope that the voices reflected in this study become part of the larger dialogue taking place on aging in U.S. society.

References

Alford, R. R., & Friedland, R. (1985). *Powers of theory.* New York: Cambridge University Press.

Almaguer, T. (1975). Class, race, and Chicano oppression. *Socialist Revolution, 5,* 71-99.

Alvirez, D., Bean, F. D., & Williams, D. (1981). The Mexican American family. In C. H. Mindel & R. W. Habenstein (Eds.), *Ethnic families in America* (pp. 269-292). New York: Elsevier.

American Association of Retired Persons. (1991). *A profile of older Americans 1990.* Washington, DC: Author.

Amott, T., & Matthaei, J. (Eds.). (1991). *Race, gender, and work: A multicultural history of women in the United States.* Boston: South End Press.

Andersen, M. L., & Collins, P. H. (Eds.). (1994). *Race, class, and gender: An anthology.* Belmont, CA: Wadsworth.

Baca Zinn, M. (1991). Contemporary structures of inequality and families. In D. S. Eitzen & M. Baca Zinn (Eds.), *Conflict and order: Understanding society* (5th ed., pp. 124-139). Boston: Allyn & Bacon.

Baca Zinn, M., & Eitzen, D. S. (1990). *Diversity in families* (2nd ed.). New York: Harper Row.

Barrera, M. (1979). *Race and class in the Southwest.* Notre Dame, IN: University of Notre Dame Press.

Becerra, R. M. (1983). The Mexican-American: Aging in a changing culture. In R. L. McNeely & J. N. Cohen (Eds.), *Aging in minority groups* (pp. 108-118). Beverly Hills, CA: Sage.

Bengston, V. L., & Burton, L. M. (1980). *Adult intergenerational relations: Effects of societal change.* New York: Springer.

Bonacich, E. (1980). Class approaches to ethnicity and race. *The Insurgent Sociologist, 10*(2), 9-23.

Boone, M. B. (1980). The uses of traditional concepts in the development of new urban roles: Cuban women in the United States. In E. Bourguignon (Ed.), *A world of women.* New York: Praeger.

Boswell, T. D., & Curtis, J. R. (1984). *The Cuban American experience.* Totowa, NJ: Rowman & Allenheld.

Brody, E., & Schoonover, C. (1986). Patterns of parent care when adult children work and when they do not. *The Gerontologist, 26,* 372-381.

Cantor, M. N. (1979). The information support system of New York's inner-city elderly: Is ethnicity a factor? In D. E. Gelfand & A. J. Kutzik (Eds.), *Ethnicity and aging* (pp. 50-61). New York: Springer.

Coles, R. (1989). *The old ones of New Mexico.* Albuquerque: University of New Mexico Press.

Cuellar, J. (1978). El Senior Citizens Club: The older Mexican-American in the voluntary association. In B. Myerhoff & A. Simic (Eds.), *Life's career-aging* (pp. 207-230). Beverly Hills, CA: Sage.

Cuellar, J. (1990). *Aging and health: Hispanic American elders* (Paper Series: No. 5). Stanford, CA: Stanford Geriatric Education Center.

Curry Rodriguez, J. E. (1988). Labor migration and familial responsibilities: Experiences of Mexican women. In M. B. Melville (Ed.), *Mexicanas at work in the United States* (Mexican American Studies Monograph No. 5). Houston: University of Houston, Mexican American Studies Program.

de la Torre, A., & Pesquera, B. (1993). *Building with our hands: New directions in Chicana studies.* Berkeley: University of California Press.

Eisenstein, Z. (Ed.). (1979). *Capitalist patriarchy and the case for socialist feminism.* New York: Monthly Review Press.

Elsasser, N., MacKenzie, K., & Tixier y Vigil, Y. (1980). *Las mujeres: Conversations from a Hispanic community.* Old Westbury, NY: The Feminist Press.

Espin, O. M. (1992). Cultural and historical influences on sexuality in Hispanic/Latin women: Implications for psychotherapy. In M. L. Andersen & P. H. Collins (Eds.), *Race, class, and gender: An anthology* (pp. 141-146). Belmont, CA: Wadsworth.

Facio, E., & Wallace, S. P. (1988). Moving beyond familism: Potential contributions of gerontological theory to studies of Chicano/Latino aging. In J. F. Gubrium & K. Charmaz (Eds.), *Aging, self, and community: A collection of readings* (pp. 207-224). Greenwich, CT.: JAI Press.

Fischer, D. H. (1978). *Historical and cross-cultural issues in aging: Growing old in America.* Oxford: Oxford University Press.

Fitzpatrick, J. P. (1971). *Puerto Rican Americans.* Englewood Cliffs, NJ: Prentice Hall.

Garcia, A. (1989). The development of Chicana feminist discourse, 1970-1980. *Gender & Society, 3,* 217-238.

Gebler, L., Moore, J. W., & Guzman, R. C. (1970). *The Mexican-American people, the nation's second largest minority.* New York: Free Press.

Hartmann, H. (1979). The unhappy marriage of Marxism and feminism: Toward a more progressive union. In L. Sargent (Ed.), *Women and revolution: A discussion of the unhappy marriage of Marxism and feminism* (pp. 1-41). London: Pluto Press.

Hartmann, H. (1981). The family as the locus of gender, class and political struggle: The example of housework. *Signs, 6,* 336-394.

Huckle, P. (1991). *Tish Sommers, activist and the founder of the Older Women's League.* Knoxville: University of Tennessee Press.

Jackson, J. (1985). Poverty and minority status. In M. Haug et al. (Eds.), *The physical and mental health of aged women* (pp. 409-430). New York: Springer.

Kasper, J. (1988). *Aging alone: Profiles and projections.* Baltimore, MD: The Commonwealth Fund Commission.

Keefe, S. E., Padilla, A. M., & Carlos, M. L. (1979). The Mexican American extended family as an emotional support system. *Human Organization, 38,* 144-152.

Kuhn, A., & Wolpe, A. M. (1978). *Feminism and materialism: Women and modes of production.* Boston: Routledge & Kegan Paul.

Lacayo, C. (1982, Spring). Triple jeopardy: Underserved Hispanic elders. *Generations,* p. 25.

Macklin, J. (1980). All the good and bad in this world: Women, traditional medicine, and Mexican American culture. In M. B. Melville (Ed.), *Twice a minority: Mexican American women* (pp. 127-148). St. Louis: C. V. Mosby.

Macklin, J., & de Costilla, A. T. (1979). La Virgin de Guadalupe and the American dream: The melting pot bubbles on in Toledo, Ohio. In S. West & J. Macklin (Eds.), *The Chicano experience* (pp. 111-143). Boulder, CO: Westview Press.

Maddox, G., & Riley, M. (1976). *Planning services for older people: Translating national objectives into effective programs.* Workshop held at Duke University, Center for the Study of Aging and Human Development.

Maldonado, D. (1975). The Chicano aged. *Social Work, 20,* 213-216.

Maldonado, D. (1979). Aging in the Chicano context. In D. E. Gelfand & A. J. Kutzik (Eds.), *Ethnicity and aging* (pp. 175-183). New York: Springer.

Maldonado, D. (1981, Summer). Senior volunteering in minority communities. *Generations, 5.*

Markides, K. S., Boldt, J. S., & Ray, L. A. (1986). Sources of helping and intergenerational solidity: A three-generation study of Mexican Americans. *Journal of Gerontology, 41,* 506-511.

Markides, K. S., Martin, H. W., & Gomez, E. (1983). *Older Mexican Americans: A study in an urban barrio.* Austin: University of Texas Press.

Markides, K. S., & Mindel, C. H. (1987). *Aging and ethnicity.* Newbury Park, CA: Sage.

Milkman, R. (1992). *Review essay: New research in women's labor history.* Los Angeles: Institute of Industrial Relations, UCLA.

Minkler, M., & Estes, C. (1991). *Critical perspectives on aging: The political and moral economy of growing old.* Amityville, NY: Baywood.

Mirande, A. (1977). The Chicano family: A reanalysis of conflicting views. *Journal of Marriage and the Family, 39,* 747-756.

Mirande, A., & Enriquez, E. (Eds.). (1979). *La Chicana: The Mexican American woman.* Chicago: University of Chicago Press.

Myerhoff, B. (1978). *Number our days.* New York: Simon & Schuster.

National Center for Health Statistics. (1990). *Current estimates from the National Health Interview Survey: U.S. 1989* (Vital and Health Statistics, Series 10, 176). Washington, DC: Author.

Navarro, V., & Berman, D. M. (Eds.). (1984). *Health and work under capitalism: An international perspective.* Farmingdale, NY: Baywood.

Nunez, F. (1975). *Variations in fulfillment of expectations of social interaction and morale among Mexican Americans and Anglos.* Unpublished masters thesis, University of Southern California, Los Angeles.

Perez, L. (1986). Immigrant economic adjustment and family organization: The Cuban success story examined. *International Migration Review, 20,* 4-20.

Pesquera, B. (1985). *Work and family: A comparative analysis of professional, clerical, and blue-collar Chicana workers.* PhD dissertation, University of California, Berkeley.

Pesquera, B. (1993). *Building with our hands.* Berkeley: University of California Press.

Redclift, N., & Mingione, E. (Eds.). (1985). *Beyond employment: Household, gender, and subsistence.* New York: Blackwell.

Ruiz, V. (1982). *Ucapawa, Chicanas, and the California food processing industry, 1937-1950.* PhD dissertation, Stanford University.

Sanchez-Ayendez, M. (1984). *Puerto Rican elderly women: Aging in an ethnic minority group in the United States.* PhD dissertation, University of Masschusetts at Amherst.

Sanchez-Ayendez, M. (1986). Puerto Rican elderly women: Shared meanings and informal suportive networks. In J. B. Cole (Ed.), *All American women: Lines that divide, ties that bind* (pp. 172-186). New York: Free Press.

Schmidt, A., & Padilla, A. M. (1983). Grandparent-grandchild interaction in a Mexican American Group. *Hispanic Journal of Behavioral Sciences, 5,* 181-198.

Segura, D. (1986). *Chicanas and Mexican immigrant women in the labor market: A study of occupational mobility and stratification.* PhD dissertation, University of California, Berkeley.

Sotomayor, M. (1973). *A study of Chicano grandparents in an urban barrio.* PhD dissertation, University of Denver School of Social Work.

Stanfield, J. H., II, & Dennis, R. M. (1993). *Race and ethnicity in research methods.* Newbury Park, CA: Sage.

Stanford, E. P., & Yee, D. (1991, Fall/Winter). Gerontology and the relevance of diversity. *Generations, 15,* 11-14.

Stoller, E. P., & Gibson, R. C. (Eds.). (1994). *Worlds of difference: Inequality in the aging experience.* Thousand Oaks, CA: Pine Forge Press.

Tauber, C. (1993). Diversity: The dramatic reality. In S. Bass, E. Kutza, & F. Torres-Gil (Eds.), *Diversity in aging* (pp. 1-46). Glenview, IL: Scott, Foresman.

Taylor, P. S. (1981). *Labor on the land: Collected writing, 1930-1970.* New York: Arno Press.

Tobias, C. (1987). *Identifying Anglo, Mexican-American and American Indian respondents for a study of recent widows: Suggestions for future researchers* (Working Paper). Tucson: University of Arizona, Tucson.

Torres-Gil, F. (Ed.). (1986). *Hispanics in an aging society.* New York: Carnegie.

Torres-Gil, F. (1992). *The new aging: Politics and change in America.* New York: Auburn House.

Torres-Gil, F., & Hyde, J. C. (1990). The impact of minorities on long-term care policy in California. In P. Liebig and W. Lammers (Eds.), *California policy choices for long-term care* (pp. 31-52). Los Angeles: University of Southern California Press.

Traeuber, C. (1991). Diversity: The dramatic reality. In S. Bass, E. Kutza, & F. M. Torres-Gil (Eds.), *Diversity in aging* (pp. 1-47). Glenview, IL: Scott, Foresman.

U.S. Bureau of the Census. (1989). *Projections of the population of the U.S. by age, sex, and race: 1988-2080* (Current Population Reports, Series P-25, No. 1018). Washington, DC: U.S. Department of Commerce.

U.S. Bureau of the Census. (1991). *Age, sex, and race and Hispanic origin information from the 1990 census.* Washington, DC: U.S. Department of Commerce.

U.S. Department of Labor, Bureau of Labor Statistics. (1987). *Employment and earnings* (Vol. 37). Washington, DC: Author.

U.S. House of Representatives, Select Committee on Aging. (1988). *Supplemental Security Income (SSI): Current program characteristics and alternatives for future reform.* Washington, DC: Government Printing Office.

U.S. Senate Special Committee on Aging. (1992). *Aging America: Trends and projects* (1991 ed.). Washington, DC: U.S. Department of Health and Human Services.

Velez, C. G. (1978). Youth and aging in central Mexico: One day in the life of four families of migrants. In B. Meyerhoff & A. Simic (Eds.), *Life's career-aging* (pp. 107-162). Beverly Hills, CA: Sage.

Verbrugge, L. (1985). An epidemiological profile of older women. In M. Haug, A. Ford, & M. Shaefor (Eds.), *The physical and mental health of aged women* (pp. 333-361). New York: Springer.

Wallace, S. P., & Facio, E. (1987). Moving beyond familism: Potential contributions of gerontological theory to studies of Chicano/Latino aging. *Journal of Aging Studies, 1,* 337-354.

Westat, Inc. (1989). *A survey of elderly Hispanics: Report for the Commonwealth Fund Commission on Elderly People Living Alone.* Washington, DC: U.S. House of Representatives.

Williams, N. (1990). *The Mexican American family: Tradition and change.* Dix Hills, NY: General Hall.

Zavella, P. (1987). *Women, work, and family in the Chicano community: Cannery workers of the Santa Clara Valley.* Ithaca: Cornell University Press.

Zepeda, M. (1979). Las abuelitas. *Agenda, 9,* 10-13.

Index

About the Author

Elisa Facio is a core faculty member of the Center for Studies of Ethnicity and Race in America (CSERA) at the Unversity of Colorado at Boulder, where she previously served as a faculty member in the Department of Sociology. Her areas of interest include the sociology of aging, Chicana feminist theory, and health care policy. She received her B.S. with honors in sociology from Santa Clara University and her M.A. and Ph.D. in sociology from the University of California at Berkeley. From 1988 to 1990, she was an NIA Postdoctoral Fellow at the University of California, San Francisco, under the direction of Dr. Carroll L. Estes. She has published articles on older Chicanas in the *Journal of Aging Studies, Oxford Companion to Women's Writing in the U.S.,* and the edited anthologies *Race and Ethnicity in Social Research* and *New Directions* in Chicana Studies. She is currently working on an article, "Health Care Policy Toward Chicanas: Assumptions, Values, and Implications of Medicaid," and on an edited anthology on Cuba. The latter is a collaborative project involving North American sociologists and Cuban social scientists from the University of Havana, Cuba.